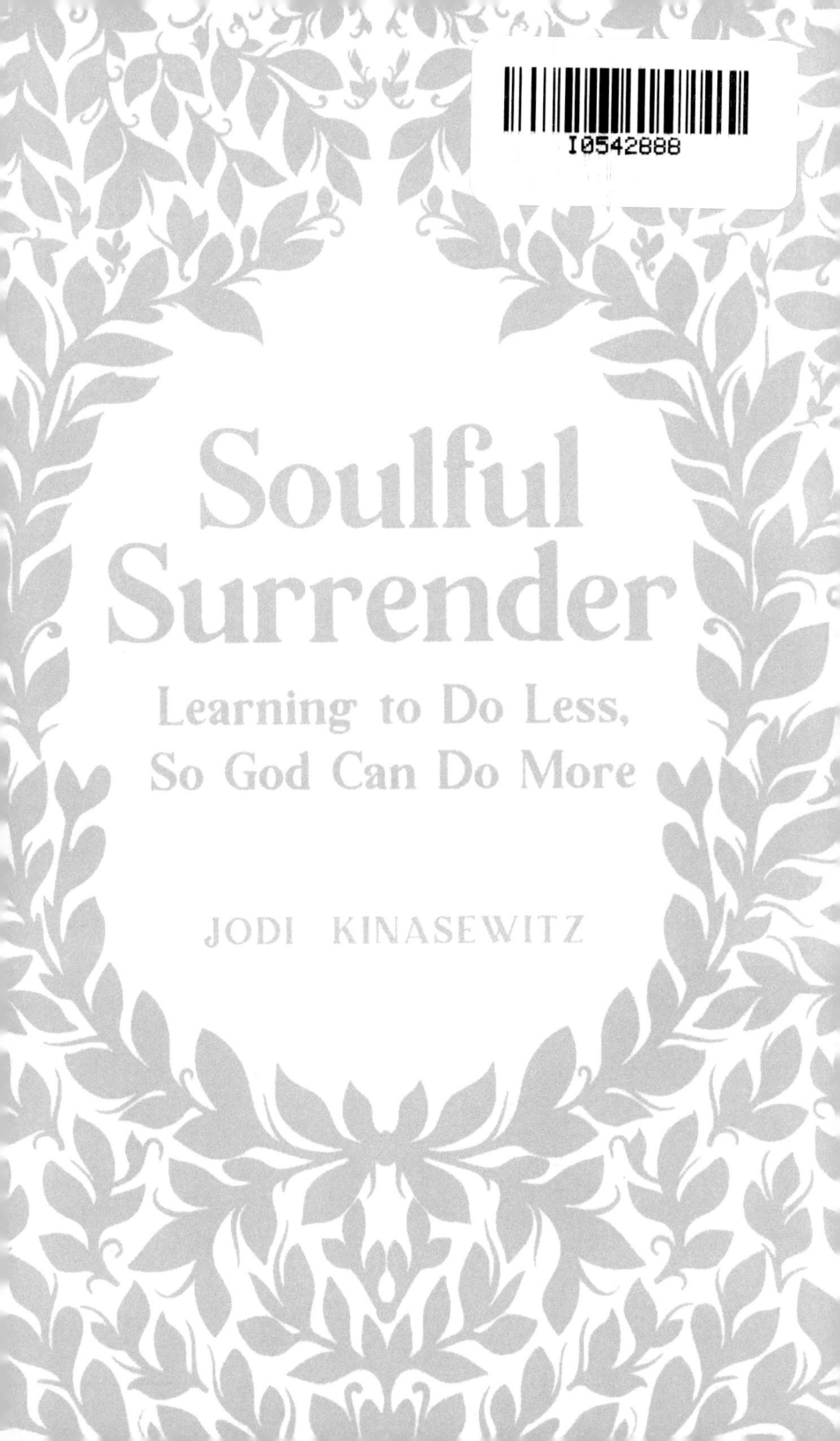

Soulful Surrender

Learning to Do Less, So God Can Do More

JODI KINASEWITZ

Soulful Surrender

Learning to Do Less,
So God Can Do More

Soulful Surrender
Copyright© 2023 by Jodi Kinasewitz

Library of Congress Cataloging-in-Publication Data

Library of Congress Number: 2023911447 | ISBN: 978-1-961732-06-3
(ebook) | ISBN: 978-1-961732-07-0 (paperback)

Published in association with Called Creatives Publishing,
www.calledcreativespublishing.com

Cover design: Called Creatives Publishing
Interior design: Jodi Kinasewitz

2023 – First Edition

Dedication

To you, the reader of this book, the one who has been sprinting on the treadmill of life and desperately wants to stop running the race. This book is your permission slip to stop striving and hustling your way through your days. As you walk through your fire (if you haven't, you will), maybe it's anxiety, depression, or something else, I pray this book reminds you that God will not allow it to ruin you. He will use it to refine you. There is beauty in our brokenness and transformation in our trials. May you hear God calling you back to His unhurried way of living and be reminded of what it looks like, and how wonderful it feels, to slow down your heart and mind and rest in Jesus. Let His light pour into you, filling you with hope, leading you all the way.

Contents

Introduction 1

Chapter 1: Less DOing, More BEing 9

Chapter 2: Less Yes, More No 25

Chapter 3: Less Self-Sufficient, More Dependent 37

Chapter 4: Less Striving, More Thriving 55

Chapter 5: Less Breaking Down, More Breaking Open 73

Chapter 6: Less Happy, More Joy 91

Chapter 7: Less Holding On, More Letting Go 103

Chapter 8: Less Fitting In, More Belonging 117

Chapter 9: Less Of Me, More Of Him 133

Chapter 10: Less About The Outcome, More About The
Becoming 151

Notes 168

Acknowledgments 170

About The Author 172

Introduction

Over the course of my life, I have been told many times that I have "a picture-perfect life" and "everything I touch turns to gold." One of my neighbors, about ten years older than me, even said, "I want to be like Jodi when I grow up." While those compliments used to give me energy and a sense of purpose, spurring me on to chase after the work-harder, do-more lifestyle, they now leave a pit in my stomach. I now know that those attributes were a result of my high-functioning anxiety and the pressure to hold everything together and excel at all costs—even the cost of my own health and the pain and suffering it put my family and me through. One can only take the pressure of living a "picture perfect" life for so long. It eventually catches up, and the end result is not so picture-perfect.

It may be hard to recognize, but those of us who seem to be the strongest and most successful are the very ones most likely needing help. The characteristics we possess and the drive we have to always perform and perfect, the things that help us achieve and experience success, are the same things that are wreaking havoc beneath the surface and masking the great pain we are in.

About six years ago, I found myself riddled with insomnia and anxiety- walking me right into a season of depression. I was tired and afraid, and I felt so lonely even though I was far from alone. My body, my mind, my soul - all were exhausted and sick and tired of being burned out from the hurry and hustle lifestyle that had somehow taken over my way of being in this world. All the years I spent stuffing away the uncomfortable feelings of doing more, I thought was what I was supposed to do—what I had to do to have a productive, successful, happy life.

I am a wife, mom of four, daughter, sister, aunt, friend, teacher, and neighbor (and, I guess, a writer). Unfortunately, I am all too familiar with that feeling of perpetual anxiety that comes from a life of constant striving and mere survival. But over the past handful of years, on a journey led by God through a season of much learning, unlearning, relearning, and growing, I've discovered a new way to live—a way that is marked by stillness, simply being, and surrendering to what God has in store for me.

> **I've discovered a new way to live—a way that is marked by stillness, simply being, and surrendering to what God has in store for me.**

And it's waking me up to how I can live fully alive. I never knew how much I needed this change, but God sure did.

Soulful Surrender shares my journey of how I learned to do less in life so that God could do more. This journey is far from over for me. This book is an invitation for you to join me on this journey. A journey that will lead you away from the constant hustle of life—the do more, be more life—and set your feet on the path of living life fully present, fully alive—doing and becoming less so that God can do and become more.

I never dreamed I would refer to "that time" in my life—my season of struggle with my mental health—as a love story, but that's exactly what it was. That's exactly what it is: a story about God's love for me, a story about how much the people in my life love me, and a story about learning to fully accept and love my imperfect self. It's a story I would never wish anyone else to have to live, but I will be forever grateful that God chose it for me. It's hands down the single most profound, life-changing story yet to be written in my life.

It was late one September night when I curled myself into a ball and, like a newborn baby, crawled onto my husband's lap and into his arms. He knew I had been experiencing a tough time—I had been suffering from extreme insomnia and daily anxiety since early that summer. We were on vacation at Disney World with the kids—a time that was supposed to be full of laughter and fun. Instead, I found myself sleep-deprived, riddled with worry over anything and everything, and sneaking off to the bathroom to cry. I was exhausted—physically, emotionally, and mentally. My body was in constant fight or flight mode, and my health was suffering. I was losing weight, suffering from constant headaches, and my body was achy and tired all of the time. My faith was flailing, and I was slipping away becoming someone who I never wanted to be. My eyes were empty, and my smiles were fake and forced. I didn't even recognize myself in the mirror.

"I can't live like this anymore," I said. "When we get home, I need to see a doctor. I'm scared, and I need help."

At this point in our lives, Matt and I had been married for sixteen years, and we had always been willing and able to support and help each other. You see, we are both doers and fixers. Something needs to be done; we do it. Something needs to be fixed; we fix it. I think that's one of the main traits that attracted us to each other—we were both get-up, get-out, and get-it-done types of people. But even Matt knew this was beyond our ability to fix. I was slipping further and further away each day. I was becoming a shell of myself. The woman who had pressed the pedal to the metal for forty-some years was coming to a full stop.

We thrived on checking every item off our to-do lists every day. This played out for the first years of our marriage as we built our house, got our master's degrees, and became nationally board certified in our respective areas of teaching. Our way of living carried over into our starting a family. We had four kids in less than six years, and we made sure to fill their days with a lot of stimulation and learning. Of course, we mastered their sleep, eat, and play schedules too. This led to finding ourselves exhausted most of the time. The whammy was double for me because I suffered from mom guilt. When I was teaching, all I could think about was how I was missing out on my babies growing up, chaperoning their field trips, volunteering in their classrooms—the list goes on and on.

Don't get me wrong; I loved my life—Matt, the kids, and my teaching career. But as content, happy, and blessed as I felt, I knew something was missing; something was off. Why else would I be so tired and stressed all the time? I knew deep down I couldn't do it all and be it all for everybody, yet something deep in me urged me on.

Something in my bones kept me living with the need to drive, push, and perform at top speed all day, every day. All the while, God was giving me signs that all was not well.

I was in a constant state of tension, jaws locked and shoulders eating my ears. I was a feelings stuffer. "I'm fine. I'm good. No, I don't need help." Yet my actions proved differently. I would huff and sigh, close (*ok, slam*) the cabinets a little too loudly, and respond irritably to Matt and the kids. I had very little patience for nonsense, and I had lost the art of goofing around. Everything had become an item to check off my list of things to do. Ignoring God's signs, I lived like this for over a decade. I trudged on, surviving each day, falling into bed, literally exhausted each night. Until God knocked on my door, got my attention, and carried me through one of the scariest seasons of my life. I wasn't listening to Him; I wasn't leaning on Him, so He brought me to a full stop.

My body, mind, and soul broke.

This book is the telling of my story, a story that looks and sounds a lot like a midlife crisis. I prefer to view it as a breaking open. The pages tell of me learning how to go from the need to be busy to be open and able to rest, from saying a thousand regretful yeses to bravely saying no, from being self-sufficient to asking for help, from gripping and controlling to letting go and surrendering, and from mindless striving and mere surviving to mindful living and thriving.

During my breaking open, I was drawn to press into God and His promises and to lean on others like never before in my life. I had a small, close-knit community of family and friends who wrapped their arms around me and walked with me through the storm. Matt and our four kids were my constants. They were a constant presence, a constant source of life and love. I hold our struggles, growth, and triumphs as a family and as individuals intimately and privately close to my heart. And they are not stories or conversations that I am ready to share. But I can share, with complete transparency, that their being—their very existence—was the driving force for me to get well. I was not about to give up on the life God had blessed me with through them, and they weren't about to let me give up on myself.

Aside from Matt and our kids, there are two other relationships that really stand out in my mind. My dad was a man of few words and certainly was not one to spend time talking on the phone. But during my dark days, though he was three hours away, he would call me almost every day. He called to check in, he called to pray with me, he directed me to certain scriptures in the Bible that had helped him in life's struggles, and he called to make sure I was getting out in the fresh air and sunshine every day. He called to tell me he loved me, he was proud of me, and that he knew things were going to get better. Aside from my own growth, healing, and transformation, the time I spent talking to my dad ended up being the most beautiful part of my story. You see, it was almost exactly a year later that we lost Dad unexpectedly. He always said, "When it's my time to go, I hope and pray it's a beautiful day and I'm working in the yard." And that's exactly where Dad was and what he was doing with the good Lord called him Home.

I look back and realize that had I not gone through my storm, I most likely would not have had the precious, heartfelt conversations I had with him. I also see God's fingerprints over all of it because while my heart shattered and life as we knew it imploded all around us, the coping skills, strategies, and strength of faith that I embodied during my breaking open helped me move forward in faith and strength at the loss of my dad. My dad held me close while I was sick and struggling, but he also saw me get better before he left for his eternal home. I still miss Dad like crazy, and I can't wait to see him again. But my faith in Jesus and knowing that Dad had faith in Him, too, makes his not being here more bearable.

The other relationship that I absolutely can't leave out of this story is the love of my sweet boy, Max, our yellow lab of 10 and a half years. As I write this very paragraph, I am drowning in sorrow over losing him just two days ago. I took him to the vet for a follow-up appointment, and with great compassion and an empathetic heart, the vet told us Max's cancer had spread all over, and he was hurting. We knew we needed to say goodbye, so through tears, belly rubs, and whispers of love in our good boy's ears, we let Max go. When I was struggling my way through my season of insomnia, anxiety, and depression, Max was a lifesaver for me–literally. He never left my side. As the saying goes, he followed me around like a little lost puppy. Max knew I was hurting–I never harmed myself, but I was afraid I might. I wanted to disappear, but Max would comfort me nestling his head in my lap as I sat in his favorite chair and cried. Through his big, brown eyes, he looked at me with wonder, joy, and tender love. He got me up and out of the house. Looking back, I know I could have easily slipped into a habit of staying in my pajamas all day. But Max, like most dogs and for sure like all labs, was too playful to just let me be. He demanded that I take him on walks and throw the ball with him. Because of Max, I got my daily dose of Vitamin D, fresh air, and exercise which I know helped in my healing.

I truly believe the saying: *from tragedy comes triumph, our tests become our testimonies, and our messes become our messages.*

This story is not an easy one. It is not a one-size-fits-all, linear path to feeling whole and being well. It was a long, arduous journey, and it still is. This story of mine is far from over. I am nowhere near the end of this journey.

I am inviting you to join me in this soulful, life-changing, challenging work. It is hard work; it is work that requires us to lose our lives and pick up the crosses Christ has given us to bear. But it is worthy work; it is work that will transform you in ways that allow you to do less

> It is hard work; it is work that requires us to lose our lives and pick up the crosses Christ has given us to bear. But it is worthy work; it is work that will transform you in ways that allow you to do less so God can do more. It is soulful surrender work.

so God can do more. It is soulful surrender work. So far, this story includes me taking ten weeks off work to seek professional medical help, seeing three different counselors, and trying four different medications until I found the one(s) that worked for me, reading countless self-help books, falling in love with reading, writing, and yoga. However, the single most important step on this journey has been my chasing Jesus and running back into His loving arms. I've fallen down many times, doubted myself and God, shamed myself for having mental health struggles, and slipped into old habits one time too many. But I've traveled far enough, and God has been with me every single step of the way. I know, without a doubt, this is how I want to live the rest of my life—a life filled with less of me and more of Him.

My prayer is that this book will help you slow down enough to tend to your heart and soul because all the hustle, hurry, and try-harder ways of life will never bring us closer to what we really need, what we really want: peace, joy, and contentment in the beautiful life God has already given us. A life that is full of everyone and everything we could ever want or need, but we are too busy trying to obtain bigger and better to notice the blessings all around us.

As you turn the pages and go on this uncomfortable and frankly unwanted journey with me, I hope you see the most important work in life is about learning to do less—to slow down, unlearn a few things, relearn some others, and let go. My life, like yours, was (and still is at times) on the runaway train this culture is obsessed with riding—produce, perform, please, and perfect. But the journey God is taking me on shows me that all I really need to do in this life is slow down– love Him and love others.

Will you join me on what is sure to be one of life's greatest journeys?

Chapter 1: Less DOing, More BEing

I am valuable, and my relationship with God, with others, and with myself is far more important than any tasks I can scratch off my to-do list.

The first time I set foot in a yoga studio was in June of 2018. I was completely out of my comfort zone. Up until that time, I had been a "doer," a "mover," a "live by my to-do list," and a "cardio to the core" kind of gal. When yoga had been mentioned or suggested to me by various people in my life over the years, I admittedly rolled my eyes and thought, "That isn't a workout." And, "Do you think I can be on a yoga mat for an hour? Hello, have you met me? Do you know me?!?!" Our jobs are never done. We are never "finished"- there will always be something else that could be, or should be, done. If you're like me (or like I was) and you tend to overdo, over-achieve, and over-schedule, this means there is never time for resting, relaxing, or replenishing. And, if we live like this for too long, burnout will find us- as it did me in 2017.

Let's go back to June of 2017 when the person I knew as myself disappeared. Self-sufficient, get it ALL done, and get it ALL done with "perfection," and without help, Jodi was gone. When I reflect on that time, I realize that I started slipping away in April of that year, but June was when my world came crashing down. I was lost; I was dark; I was scared; I was alone. Even though I, by standards of the outside world's view, had "the perfect life": faith and trust in God since childhood; a loving husband; four healthy, happy kids; amazing friends; a secure job; great relationships with parents, my brother, and other extended family members. I had it "all." Until I didn't. Over the summer of 2017, what started with a sense of being on edge and suffering from insomnia, quickly turned to paralyzing anxiety and crippling depression. I could not, for the life of me, find myself. It spiraled because I realized rather quickly that I needed help, but I had never asked for help (nothing of real significance, anyway) from anyone for anything in my life. And, I questioned my faith... "God, I love you, I trust you, give me the strength to handle this passing phase without pausing to ask for help or have to get help." I questioned my faith, and this literally broke me. "If I am a true believer, I can handle this. I've got this," I thought. "I don't need counseling; I don't need medication; I don't need help... I don't. I don't." I don't was all I said, until one day I realized... I did. I did need help; I did need to take the recommended medications; I did need to take time away from work to find myself again; I did need to seek counseling; I did need to be open to other "out there" self-care tools (insert yoga, meditation, journaling, etc.). And I definitely needed to get back to making my time with Jesus a top priority. I needed to rebuild and reclaim my somewhat complacent faith with faith in Him like a child.

Up to this point in my life, I was self-sufficient. Looking back now, I see with eyes wide open that I was passive and complacent, especially in my faith life. The alarm would go off at 5 AM. I would jump out of bed, drink (*ok, chug*) a cup of coffee, crank through my workout, get showered for work, get the kids out the door, head to teach 8th-grade special education students, come home, fix dinner–maybe actually sit and eat it– while doing the laundry and managing the homework thing, shuffle kids to sporting events and other activities, get everyone in bed, settle myself for the next morning, and then in the blink of an eye......BUZZZ! BUZZZ! BUZZZ! The alarm would sound at 5 AM, and I'd hit the repeat button. Like many others, my go-to response when asked, "How are you?" was the automatic "Good!, Just busy!". I was "doing" life, but

I wasn't "living" life. A life of love, joy, contentment, and peace is what I craved more than anything else. A life like the heart of Jesus. But I was in too big of a hurry.

All the running around and hustling didn't get me anywhere except in a state of exhaustion. I felt important and worthy because my days were jam-packed with activity. My busy was hiding my anxiety. When I have control of things, or at least I think I do, it makes me feel less anxious. My constant state of controlling and doing left no time for me to notice, recognize, or feel my anxiety. I would stuff all the feelings down, push them aside, and tell myself, 'Nobody has time for that.' I thought my days were productive and purposeful, but all I was doing was checking boxes on my to-do list. Being busy felt important, but what was it I was really building? I was all about the badge of honor that comes with "being busy." And it wasn't just me– many of my "mom" friends were alongside me on that non-stop runaway train because society tells us that productivity and busyness make us worthy. Productivity gives us a sense of purpose, meaning, and achievement. And, for me, it was a way to escape or avoid what I was really feeling.

When October 2017 rolled around, I crashed...hard! I was powering through my days in typical Jodi fashion–ignoring what was going on with me and telling myself to "just deal with it." But, I could not carry on. My body literally, physically, mentally, and emotionally broke down. My loving, empathetic boss at the time, as well as my husband and parents, encouraged me to take some time to rest, rejuvenate, and reflect on what I needed to do to get better, to feel better. While I was in the midst of this storm: time off work, finding a counselor that I connected with, getting just the right dose and combination of medicines, and finally getting some much-needed sleep, I was also gifted with an everyday connection with my dear Dad. My parents live about three hours from me, so while they could not be with me physically every day I walked through this storm, they were with me in every other sense. My dad, in particular, was my lifeline. He was retired, so he would call every day to check in with me, encourage me, remind me to keep fighting, look for the good, and see the good. My anticipation of Dad's call, the phone ringing, and our talks got me through a lot of very difficult days. I was not only afforded extra time with Dad, but I also had nothing but time on my hands, so I turned more intentionally to my heavenly father and His word. The scripture and time in prayer were water for my soul; it was healing, and I know it is, in the end, what saved me. Both of my fathers were speaking to me, and telling me that I mattered, that I had a life worth living (actually being, not just doing), and that I had a purpose. I vividly remember pleading and crying out to God, "Why am I going through this? What are you preparing me for? Is something big going to happen that you need to make me stronger now, so I can handle it?" I wanted answers to the reason behind this storm. Another lesson I needed to learn; we don't always get the answers. That is what "letting go" is all about.

By January 2018, I was back to teaching; I was coming to terms with the fact that medications were acceptable; I was attending a counseling session every week; I was open about my mental health struggles with the most important people in my life, including my four children, and I was feeling a bit more like myself. Thankfully, that identity of who I was had drastically changed. I was no longer self-sufficient, I was appropriately dependent on the wonderful people God had placed in my life, and I was drawn to time well spent with God like no other time in my life. God, and His word, were now my morning wake-up call. I was less judgmental; I was more focused on being present rather than perfect. I was on my way back.

Fast forward to June of 2018 when I walked into this warm, inviting, cool vibe yoga studio— remember yoga was that thing, that "exercise" that I scoffed at a year before. Well, the moment I stepped foot in the door, I was welcomed. I was appreciated. I was seen. I was important. I mattered. I have, not even once, looked back or thought about letting my yoga go. The "Come as you are, all are welcome, let go, smile, breathe, judgment-free zone" that is the atmosphere of this studio and, in fact, the entire philosophy of yoga, in general, has saved me. More than that, yoga has helped me find a me that I didn't realize existed. Yoga has taught me to slow down, even stop. Yoga has taught me that the practice, and therefore life itself, is just that– a practice; no perfection necessary. When I am on my mat, I get lost in myself. My hopes and dreams feel real. I feel good. I feel free. I feel worthy and deserving. When in yoga class, the internal connection is so deep. But, BUT... the connection to the greater good of this world, the connection to the other humans in that class, lights a fire in my soul. I hear the breath of others as I concentrate on my breath; I see the falling out of poses and the struggle of balance in others as I struggle to hold my Warrior 3 pose. In yoga class, I feel and see patience and persistence; I feel and see grit and grace; I hear the instructor saying, "Let go, breathe, be kind to yourself, surrender." And these feelings, these emotions, elicit something in me that lets me know that even if the storm comes, and it will; even if life knocks me down, and it will; I can get back up again, and again, and again! My first few classes of yoga consisted of me releasing a lot of tears and being in constant prayer with God. I felt God's presence in the quiet and stillness of my resting pose every time. Yoga is an exercise practice that taught me how to slow down, and it helped reinstall my faith, hope, and trust in God because, in my season of despair, my yoga mat was the only place where I could be still enough to find Him.

In November of 2018, my world did come crashing down in a way that I wasn't sure I could, or would, be able to get back up. But this time, it was loss, real loss–emotional loss, mental loss, and physical loss. My dad, my rock, my go-to person over the past tumultuous year, unexpectedly passed away. We were stunned, numb. Our family is so close, and Dad was the rock. Our compass of common sense, our source of unconditional love, our truest example of loving and living without limits or regrets. So you see, my self-reflection, my willingness to hit the pause button on life, my agreement to seek counseling and consider medication, my time spent talking with Dad, his more than normal frequent visits, my soul searching and digging deep into my faith and God's Word, my realization that this life is meant to be lived, not simply done, were all huge catalysts for my healing. And they prepared me, giving me strength and armor to help me stand strong and prevail through the devastating storm of losing Dad.

And yoga. My yoga mat became a place where I could sit quietly with my thoughts of Dad, oftentimes dedicating my practice to him and crying my way through the poses. Yoga, like Dad, has helped me realize that there is no perfection, there is no endpoint, and there is no isolation. Yoga, in itself, means to join or unite. For me, this means uniting my body, mind, and soul with God. I quickly learned that yoga is not simply stretching and becoming successful. Yoga is digging deep to examine yourself. Yoga is taking the time to be present for yourself and others. Yoga is asking for help when needed. Yoga is a lifelong journey– it is a practice, not perfection. I know that I will continually learn and grow— emotionally, physically, and spiritually as I continue my yoga journey.

After a year of deep spiritual and personal growth, I decided that if yoga made me feel so good and it is where I felt completely quiet and connected to God, more than at any other time in my life, then I wanted to share this joy, this acceptance, this transformative practice with others. So, I decided to take a Yoga Teacher Training course. I wanted to bring this journey and share this connection of thoughts, actions, and feelings with someone else. I want to help others see that yoga helps you see the testimonies in tests and the messages in the messes of life. And my long-term goal was to become certified and lead a Christian-based yoga class. I brought this idea, this dream, before God in January 2018. I completed my certification course and began teaching yoga in the summer of 2018. I continued to present God with my hope of being given the opportunity to teach a Christian-based class. I prayed with Him, I believed in His timing, and I waited patiently for the opportunity to present itself. I wanted to share my love of Jesus with others through the practice of yoga. And, friend God is good. He opened the door for me and my dream. I started teaching Faithful Flow, a Christian-based yoga class, in January 2019.

In short, I am learning every day that yoga, like my spiritual life, is a journey of practice, not perfection. I will stumble. I will fall. I will lose my balance. I may even feel lost at times. But, I will always, always have my breath—the breath and mercies that God gives me new every morning. And with God's strength, I will always get up from every fall. I will learn to accept who I am, where I am, with what I have on any given day. I will be knocked down many more times in my life, but the faithful presence of the Holy Spirit inside of me will whisper, "Jodi, get up! Get Up! Get Up! Get Up! And, Get On Your Mat!"

While I had been working on myself– doing the hard work of tuning into my thoughts, feelings, emotions, and needs—through counseling and my own self-study, my yoga practice is what really opened my eyes to the value and vital need to be in tune with myself enough to recognize my thoughts, accept them, and then send them on their way if they weren't serving me in a positive way. Yoga became a time and place where my body and mind became so still, so quiet that it was the first place I felt I could truly feel the presence of God and hear the Holy Spirit whispering to me. I had been living a life where busyness was a way for me to be distracted and deny my feelings. The inability to sit with myself, notice my feelings, observe them, and study them, was not serving me well. I was not proving anything to anyone, albeit I thought I was. My constant state of striving, firing on all cylinders in an independent, self-sufficient way, was just me being chockful of pride and anxiety. I was spinning so fast that I didn't even realize that my physical, mental, and emotional exhaustion was my own doing. I had taken away my body's right to be a human BEING, and I had replaced it with the false satisfaction of success through constant DOING and producing.

I had taken away my body's right to be a human BEING, and I had replaced it with the false satisfaction of success through constant DOING and producing.

15

Looking back, it is so crystal clear– so easy for me to see– that I was living a life keeping myself busy, always looking ahead to the next challenge, as a way to ignore and continue stuffing down my own feelings. Sure, I was living life, but I don't know that I can honestly say I was enjoying life. I was disconnected from myself, I was distant from God, and I was in complete denial that I needed, and deep down wanted, help. I wanted to be a super-woman, super-wife, super-mom, and super-teacher. I just kept running on the wheel, getting nowhere. I was avoiding the uncomfortable, awkward recognition that my soul needed tending. Boy, did it ever, but I didn't want to admit it.

All the effort and time I was putting into learning and doing would have been better spent on living life more fully and experiencing growth that comes with setbacks, do-overs, and failures. I had to learn the hard way that my value is not based on how I perform, achieve, or produce. My body, and my mind, were giving me all the signals– they were screaming at me to stop and rest. And the rest I was finally forced to take, thanks be to God, reminded me that I, in and of myself, am worthy. I am valuable, and my relationship with God, with others, and with myself is far more important than any tasks I can scratch off my to-do list.

Friends, even Jesus rested. He found value in and actively sought alone time. We read several times in Scripture where Jesus found and took time for solitude and quiet space. In the Book of Mark, we read about how He made time to be at rest with His Father and God renewed His strength, "Very early in the morning, while it was still dark, Jesus got up, left the house and went off to a solitary place, where he prayed" (Mark 1:35). We too must prioritize rest. What's stopping you from taking time to rest? Whatever it is, I promise it won't matter ten years from now- it may not even matter ten hours from now. You must pick a time to rest, or like me, your body will pick one for you. I believe God used my struggle with insomnia, anxiety, and depression as a spiritual wake-up call. He saw that I was continuing down the slippery slide of self-sufficiency and pride, and He knew He needed to intervene. He needed to get my attention, and He did.

He reminded me, "Be still, and know that I am God" (Psalm 46:10). As He took me on this spiritual journey—which to me felt like a complete mid-life crisis. He taught me that I can't rush past the feelings. Similar to all other facets of my life, I wanted answers and quick fixes. My hurried state of living made it difficult for me to take the time to sit with my feelings and reflect on what may be causing them. God used this time to restore me and refine me. He wanted me to examine myself, my true self, not the self I had slapped five thousand social and cultural labels on. God wanted me to examine the masterpiece He had made me to be.

Living through difficulty—times of loneliness, grief, overwhelm, weariness, and so on—is easily equated to the harshness of winter. Most of us dread the long, dark, bitterly cold days of winter. We wish them away in an attempt to rush to spring, where all is bright and new again. But just as the change of seasons is inevitable, so too are we certain to face some sort of physical, emotional, mental, or spiritual winter. These are not seasons of life that we would ever choose to come to face with, but if we live long enough, they will most certainly come. But there is hope during these winter seasons. We do know that, like the coming and going of the seasons, our trouble times will also pass. As Jennifer Dukes Lee writes in her book *Growing Slow*, "But what if winter is more than a season to be tolerated until we arrive somewhere better? What if winter is more than a required passageway to reach the prize of spring? Winter is not just a doorway; it is a room all its own, with treasures to be discovered and pondered. Looking back, I can see that the winter seasons of my life grew me in ways I didn't know I needed at the time. They grew faith inside of me that I never imagined possible. In my heart's coldest winters, I learned about perseverance, patience, and endurance, traits that would serve me well in the summers of my heart." [1] Well, this was my winter season or at least one of them. I had pushed away, forced down, and ignored the changes and work God was trying to do in and through me, so He had to place me smack dab in the middle of a cold, dark, scary season. Most days this season did not have sunny skies or answers and fixes wrapped beautifully with a bow on top. Most days felt lonely, exhausting, and insurmountable. But, He got me through, and with each day, I grew a bit stronger and more resilient. He was growing something beautiful in the dark, cold, rocky soil of my soul's tumultuous time. What felt like a season of death became a renewal of life–my life. My body and mind forced me to retreat and rest. I had to turn inward, quieting my mind and soul.

> He was growing something beautiful in the dark, cold, rocky soil of my soul's tumultuous time. What felt like a season of death became a renewal of life-my life.

How did my resiliency grow? By doing the only thing, I felt I could do—spending time in prayer and in God's word. During this dark winter season, when it felt as if the whole world was happily moving along and I was becoming a shell of myself, God was at work. He was pulling me in, showing me with His tender loving care that I needed to slow down and let Him tend the fields of my heart and soul. With each day, I learned to let my season be the life lesson that it was. I stopped wishing it away and asking God all the "Why me?" questions, and I began to view it as a journey. I looked at it as a path I was traveling that was going to lead me to places I had never been. It was leading more toward a more surrendered way of life. So as shared in 2 Corinthians, I did not lose heart. While outwardly I was wasting away–loss of weight, dark circles under my eyes, a ghost-like appearance with no life or light in my eyes– inwardly, God was renewing me day by day.

I was learning that the struggle I was facing and walking through each day was more than just a season; it was a gift all by itself. I would never have grown the way I did—spiritually, emotionally, and relationally—had God not taken me through this storm. In this winter-like season, I gained perspective, patience, persistence, perseverance, and endurance. These were attributes that I didn't have before, or at least I was not aware of how deeply I possessed them. Perspective to see that life is not all about the hustle and the tangible rewards. Patience to get to know me, to see myself and all my beautifully blemished ways, patience to find a doctor and counselor that aligned with my spiritual beliefs, persistence to keep trying medications even after some of them made me feel like I was crawling out of my skin. Perseverance and endurance to get up every morning, one dark day after another, pursue my wellness, and fight for my life, my happiness, and my family. These traits will continue to serve me well in other seasons filled with strife and in the full embrace and enjoyment of the lighter, sunnier seasons.

When I walked away from my teaching job in October 2017, I had no other choice. My body was shutting down. I was running on very little gas, more like fumes. I was crawling and crying my way through every day. I literally could not dig deep, pull myself up by my bootstraps, put my big girl pants on, and power through. While I had always been one to avoid the uncomfortable, to fight and power through because I don't like sitting, waiting, and being still, it was so hard and so painfully slow. I wanted what I thought had always worked for me–the quick and dirty "how to" fixes and lists. Tell me the five things I should do to get a good night's sleep; show me how I can breathe to help calm myself down; give me a list of ways to avoid anxiety. But I was coming to realize that I couldn't fix this on my own, and it was becoming apparent that no one could fix it for me. Because you see, I didn't need to be "fixed," and neither do you. When we face tough times, we don't need to be fixed. We need help.

When we face tough times, we don't need to be fixed. We need help.

For the first time in my life, after four decades of being the doer and the helper, I knew I needed help, and I asked for it. I realized that this season I was in was not going to go away quietly. I needed to face it, accept it, and embrace it. I was learning that life doesn't skip over the hard stuff. If I wanted to make a change, if I wanted to feel differently, if I wanted a better way of living, then I knew I had to put in the hard work. And the first step of that work was being still. Sitting with myself, my thoughts, and my feelings, and being open to them, accepting of them, and loving them.

Our best contribution to our families, friends, workplaces, churches, etc., is ourselves. If we don't take care of ourselves and make ourselves and our health—physical, mental, emotional, and relational— a priority, we will fail others, and even worse, we'll fail ourselves. Prioritizing our doing over our being will lead to burnout and a breaking down of our productivity. For me, the first thing to go when I feel the need to perform and produce is rest—not actual sleep but just simply sitting down and resting my mind and my body. I have often let my Type A, ambitious personality and need to succeed take over. Instead of pacing myself, listening to my body and cloudy mind, I have powered through, and the end result has been far from thriving—it has been mere survival. The challenge for me is not that I need to work harder; rather, it is I need to NOT work harder; I need to stop striving, reaching, and doing. I have always been one to value sleep. I had always gone to bed at a decent time but often would toss and turn and not get real rest due to the numerating thoughts spinning in my mind. It wasn't until I ~~broke down~~ broke open that I learned to value rest. At all. I looked at those who napped, sat on the couch to read, watched tv, or just stared off as lazy, unproductive, and unmotivated. I was tired—All. The. Time. I have now learned to value the need and beauty of rest, a true Sabbath. I honor it. I value it. I make it a priority, and I no longer feel emotionally and physically exhausted like I did for years. God did not create anything with the intention to produce 24/7. There are rhythms of rest all throughout the Bible. There are rhythms of rest all around us—the moon, stars, nature, seasons, etc. No matter who or what it may be, everything flourishes and is bigger and brighter when it takes time to stop and rest.

> **No matter who or what it may be, everything flourishes and is bigger and brighter when it takes time to stop and rest.**

I finally realized that I had to stop all the doing and eliminate much of the input in order to increase my truly valuable output. All I was doing was reacting. Now, with my slower space, a calmer mind and body, and a lessened sense of urgency, I find myself more reflective and more responsive. If we slow down our pace and stop and ask ourselves how much time we are actually saving by working so frantically, we will ease our heaviness of exhaustion. In order to create great output, we must stop useless input—social media scrolling, comparing ourselves to others, and working to perform, perfect, and please—otherwise, we're just reacting. I don't know about you, but I was worn out because I was failing to love who and what was present and choosing to love what was possible. We have this unhealthy habit and tendency to slip into a constant state of seeking, working, doing, living, and striving for the next best thing. The perfect vacation, perfect party, perfect paperwork, and meeting somehow, often unknowingly, take precedence over our being present in the current moment–present to the day and people that are right before us.

Don't get me wrong; it's okay to want more, to think about our tomorrows and the love that will exist—that all just means we're human and we're living. We can't always be in this exact moment. Mindfulness is not going to take away our tomorrows. And I know full well that life is busy. It just is. There is no denying it. But I also know there is time to take breaks, to pause, to just be. When I find myself with a full schedule and a long to-do list, I purposefully plan pauses. I take a walk during my lunch break, I do a few simple yoga poses in between tasks, and I am sure to get outside for a blast of fresh air. In *Growing Slow,* Jennifer Dukes Lee urges us to "un-hurry our hearts." She goes on to encourage her reader when she says, "Let's see the winter not as something that must be endured, but something that must be treasured. God will

Step into each season with trust, faith, and hope in God that it is the exact season you need in order for Him to do His work in and through you.

use winter seasons to grow us." [2] So friends, I urge you to slow down too. Step into each season with trust, faith, and hope in God that it is the exact season you need in order for Him to do His work in and through you. You can hold your present season and, at the same time, find yourself living for what might be, what is possible, and loving those ideas and dreams means that we are living, and I do want more of that. I want more of God. Don't you?

I now value the idea of simply being. I start my day by getting quiet and reflecting on who I am, how I am feeling at that moment, whom God says I am, and how He feels about me. I am more comfortable now than ever before in my life. I am more comfortable with myself when I strip away all my titles– wife, mom, daughter, sister, teacher, friend, neighbor, writer– and I discover the joys, delights, passions, and gifts God has given me. I have learned that it's better to slow down rather than break down. It's better to do less and let God do more.

> **I have learned that it's better to slow down rather than break down. It's better to do less and let God do more.**

Scripture

Psalm 46:10 *"He says, 'Be still, and know that I am God; I will be exalted among the nations, I will be exalted in the earth.'"*

Reflection

In what areas of your life do you find yourself always "doing"? How can you find stillness throughout your day? What thoughts, activities, commitments, etc., are stealing your stillness? Where or how can you fit pockets of time to be still in your day?

_____

_____

_____

_____

Prayer

Lord, I know I need to be still. In this noisy world, I am trying to find stillness. Help me to quit moving about and shift my focus to you alone. I crave being able to find a state of stillness rather than being scattered and having my focus all over the place.

Chapter 2: Less Yes, More No

Lean on God for the courage to say "No" by focusing less on the needs of others and more on what He has in store for you.

No. A word I wish I had learned years ago. Is it upsetting that it took an ~~emotional breakdown~~ spiritual wake-up call for me to realize that I had to start using the word 'no' more often…yes, perhaps. Do I wish I had learned to use the word "no" more freely back in my teens, twenties, and early Mom years? 100% Yes! Do I regret how I came to my current understanding of how liberating the word "no" can be for my well-being? Well, honestly… No.

My season of anxiety and depression taught me that I was spending all my time, all my energy, and all my "yeses," proving myself to others and proving my love for them. I have learned that I have nothing to prove. I am worthy—just me, just the way I am. My yeses and noes have nothing to do with my value. I have learned to simplify my life by living in a more uncomplicated way. It's not always easy, but I am learning to make things simpler by removing all the complications, conflict, turmoil, and unease inside of me by saying no when I want to instead of pretending it's a yes. For years I said yes when deep down I really was feeling big, hard noes. I am making my outward choices match my inside, my heart. I get it. It can be scary to say no. Saying no is vulnerable; it exposes your true thoughts and feelings. But I would give anything to have been brave enough to be vulnerable when my kids were younger. I would have benefited, and so would they have, from me saying no more often and modeling that saying no, and going after what your heart wants and what God is calling you to do, can disappoint others- and that's ok.

Having four kids in less than six years certainly created a packed-to-the-brim calendar in our house. Matt and I wanted the kids to be able to experience and be involved in as many activities as we could manage. The thing is, because we are both over-doers, and we have no family living near us, the well-intentioned activities had the two of us running ragged. The constant hustle and hurry from drop-offs to pick-ups and leaving one field to race to another, most often having breakfast and or lunch packed in a cooler because we would leave our house at 8 AM on Saturday mornings and often not get home until 4 or 5 PM. We were in a constant yes mode, never willing to ask for help because we, especially me, wanted to appear as if we had it all together. As a mom and full-time teacher, I carried a lot of mommy guilt. I hated that I couldn't volunteer at the kids' schools, go in and read to their classes, help chaperone the field trips, be the room mom, etc. This was doubly hard for me because most of the kids' friends' moms did stay home, and they could be at the schools for all the special happenings. This made me feel less than others. The kids never said anything, and the other moms never once made me feel bad, not even for a second, but I put that on myself. I told myself I was less than others. And since I couldn't do all the things during the school day hours, I made sure to sign up and volunteer for everything under the sun during the evening hours and on my summer break. I was a cheer coach, a vacation Bible school teacher, a nursery worker, and a volunteer for play productions, and you better believe I was the first to click the "signup" button on every SignUp Genius that came from the schools. All of my yeses were about proving myself to be a good mom and proving my love to my kids.

The thing is, I already was a good mom, and the kids knew (and still know) that I love them more than life itself. I did this all on what was supposed to be my "off" time—my time to rest, recoup, and rejuvenate. I put all the pressure on myself to get involved, to do more, and to be everything to everybody. Deep down, I wanted to say no to many of these things because every time I was gone spending my time doing an activity for one of the kids, I felt immediate guilt about leaving the others. But again, I did this to myself. I was saying yes instead of no because I doubted myself, my intentions, and my worth. I was always looking to prove myself. So with all my yeses came a lot of people pleasing. I was doing what others felt was important rather than listening to myself and what I thought was important. I guess you could say I had a case of "FOMO." I held fear that I would miss out on something fun— some amazing opportunity or experience. Now, I rest easy in what some call "JOMO," or the joy of missing out. I don't carry the worry over burning bridges, creating tension, letting others down, etc. I feel confident that, for the most part, my noes are good noes, and my yeses are full and whole-hearted—which people prefer over half-hearted yeses any day.

In order for me to understand the importance of employing the word no on a more consistent basis, I had to first become anxiety aware. I was living in a constant state of anxiety; I just didn't recognize it as such. To understand the importance and beauty of the word no, I learned how to be less anxious. I had to learn how to just be, how to create calm and stillness. I also had to recognize that the practices of being calm and becoming still were not fruitless. They were not about me sitting around, twiddling my thumbs, and doing nothing. I had to let go of the perception that if I was still, I was worthless. I had to learn and grow and stretch and realize that being still, being

> **I had to let go of the perception that if I was still, I was worthless.**

calm, and being quiet is about clearing the clutter—getting rid of all the trash-talking that goes on my mind. I have a feeling you know what I'm talking about. We just keep saying yes, and our stress levels and mental health suffer because of it.

Through learning to quiet my mind and my body—thank you very much, yoga—I was able to free up mental and emotional space to feel, think, question, and dream big dreams. I was able to tap into myself— my thoughts, my feelings, my desires, my interests, and my passions. Friend, I have learned that if saying yes takes away from the time and energy I need to do things that I enjoy doing and that are more important to me, then saying no is always the better choice. It's the better choice for you too.

I had ignored my feelings of anxiety by staying in a constant state of busyness. I would stay anxious by trying to stay ahead of becoming anxious. I had anxiety over having anxiety. Can you relate? I know you can. A phrase I often hear and couldn't agree more with, even though I don't know who originally coined it, is, "This world needs more time to do less and be less." Everyone take a breath, slow down, maybe even stop. We need to stop, stare, and soak in our everyday moments more. When we stop and stare, when we stop and wonder, when we stop and get curious when we stop and think, and when we stop and question, we begin to internalize. If we're not careful, if we're not more mindful, if we're not more present to what is happening around us, the moments, the feelings, and the emotions will wash over us, and we will look back and remember very little. We need to bring these moments- the small, ordinary, mundane, hard, good, bad, ugly moments- into ourselves. Breathe them in as if they are the air we need to survive.

As I first started transitioning into this person whose noes meant no so that my yeses could be more powerful and more meaningful, it was a bumpy ride. I felt like I was living a life where nothing was happening. The feeling of worthlessness for my days and my lack of activity kept creeping in. We all have the desire to contribute and be fruitful. So, like I am sure it is for you, it was hard for me to keep saying the noes and feeling like I had accomplished next to nothing at the end of each day. But I came to realize that every season is not a growing season. I was planting a harvest. I began to notice what was changing, what was developing beneath the surface—my relationships, my rested mind, my

> But I came to realize that every season is not a growing season. I was planting a harvest.

connectedness, my joy, and my energy had all begun to flourish. I learned that it's not always my time to shine. I was enjoying this time to sit it out; I was thriving in the beauty and time God was giving me to rest. I grew and found new interests that showed me kindness in what I called this "unproductive" mode. I learned that I found joy and rest in simply being with my family and hanging out with no agenda and no plan. I found joy in reading, writing, and yoga. I found happiness in a season of "not" doing.

Once I started saying no to all the things, I found that I was able to better tune in to my daily happenings and my loved ones. While the slowing down did bring about some discouragement and disappointment, I slowly began to realize that this was a much-needed, very important step in my journey to becoming the very best version of myself. Getting to a place of being at peace with the slowness, the stillness, and the stagnancy, I will admit, took time. I did not feel light, free, and excited with anticipation when my journey first began. No, I was frustrated, scared, angry, uncertain, and barely keeping my head above water. To even begin to think clearly and make decisions about how to best move forward, to begin to introduce more fun and play into my life, I needed sleep. I needed rest. And I learned that if my 'noes' disappoint others, well then…oh well.

Oh, how I wish I would have had author and researcher Brene Brown's written works in my hands long before I did. In her book, *The Gifts Of Imperfection,* Brown speaks to the heart of the matter when she quotes the work of psychiatrist and clinical researcher Dr. Stuart Brown when he argues that play is not an option. In fact, he says, "The opposite of play is not work—the opposite of play is depression." [1] This could not ring more true to the state I had found myself in. I had given up on play.

I had deep-dived into a lifestyle of working hard, hustling all day, and stopping when you drop mentality. In her book, Brown explains that if we truly want to live wholeheartedly, we have to become intentional about cultivating sleep and play, and we have to let go of exhaustion as a status symbol and productivity as self-worth. This was a hard lesson for me to learn- but, boy, was it necessary. I had to learn that it is okay to say no. I discovered new ways to be kind and courteous in my 'no' responses without sacrificing my sense of self-worth. I had to decide if I was going to continue to live in a hurried state or if I wanted to be more mindful of my time. Do you know what I noticed when I started saying no more often? Life went on anyway— activities, school events, teams, clubs, meetings, etc., all continued to move along whether I was there or not.

> **Your "no" will not have devastating impacts on the lives of others, but if you don't allow yourself the grace to say no every once in a while, it may have a devastating impact on you.**

And the same holds true for you, friend. Your "no" will not have devastating impacts on the lives of others, but if you don't allow yourself the grace to say no every once in a while, it may have a devastating impact on you.

God had things to do in my soul. He still does; I am sure of it. And because He was trying to do work in me that I was not interested in, He took me through a season of struggle, a season of waiting. He kept me in the dark on purpose. He made me crawl when all I ever wanted to do was run. He teaches us, "Come to me, all you who are weary and burdened, and I will give you rest" (Matthew 11:28).

I am learning more every day and could not agree more with Brown when, in her book *The Gifts of Imperfection,* she says, "Wholehearted living is about engaging in our lives from a place of worthiness. It means cultivating the courage, compassion, and connection to wake up in the morning and think, 'No matter what gets done and how much is left undone, I am enough.' It's going to bed at night thinking, 'Yes, I am imperfect and vulnerable and sometimes afraid, but that doesn't change the truth that I am also brave and worthy of love and belonging.'" [2] I am so grateful that God got my attention and taught me to realign my priorities—He taught me, that while I felt the societal, and cultural pressure to keep saying a thousand yeses, taking the step to start saying my first noes may have seemed small and meaningless and even regrettable at the time, but the ripple effects of these small, seemingly meaningless noes have released extraordinary ripple effects. First, I don't feel utterly exhausted all the time. Secondly, by saying no, I free up space for others to step up and get involved. If we are always the ones saying yes, how in the world do we expect others to have the opportunity to get involved? Remember, just because you are available to do something or you have the skills to do something, doesn't mean it should be an automatic yes. I have grown into a habit of wait-and-seeing when I am asked to do something. Rather than immediately saying yes, I take the time to really process what I'm saying yes to. I reflect on what kind of commitment it is, and on whether it is something I really want to do or something I feel I should do. By saying no, we are showing people that we are taking care of ourselves, that it's okay for them to do the same, and we are modeling the way of Christ.

When I say "no," I am being like Jesus. Jesus said no, and he created clarity by letting his yes be yes, and his

> **When I say "no", I am being like Jesus.**

no be no. He went off in solitude and prayed; he set boundaries and provided us with guidance. "All you need to say is simply 'Yes' or 'No'; anything beyond this comes from the evil one" (Matthew 5:37). I can see in His word how His noes show that when we see our limitedness, that is a good thing. It is not one bit selfish. By choosing my noes carefully, my yeses carry much greater meaning and joy. When I consciously and prayerfully choose not to do something, I am also consciously and fully choosing TO do something else. It matters that much more. It is such a comforting feeling to know that I am saying yes because I want to and because God wants me to. We need to tune into our bodies and listen up. Saying yes to the tugs on your heart or that feeling deep in your stomach is saying yes to the Holy Spirit. As a giver, I have to remember to learn my limits because the takers—people, activities, and to-dos in my life—don't have any. I used to carry so much guilt about taking time for myself. While I highly doubt this to be true because people don't think about us as much as we think they do (they have their own stuff to worry about), I felt like I was being judged by other moms and wives when I would step away from the demands of daily life to catch my breath and treat myself. But, then I reminded myself that even Jesus took time and said "yes" to developing himself and his potential when "After three days they found him in the temple courts, sitting among the teachers, listening to them and asking them questions" (Luke 2:46). My struggle with anxiety and depression taught me that if I don't take care of myself, my health, my body, and more importantly my mind and soul would suffer. If we don't tend to the gardens of our hearts, how do we expect to produce a harvest? How do we expect to grow beautiful things? Why would we think we would bear much fruit?

How do we do this, you ask? When do we have time? Where do we go? What do we do? This is where the hard work comes in. This is when you have to roll up your sleeves and get your hands moving—dig in and do all the work that you do to meet the needs of others—your husband, your kids, your friends, and your coworkers. And work for you as you work for them. Sit with yourself as you sit with them, ask yourself what you want as you ask them, and listen to yourself as you listen to them.

Stop obsessing over your outer life-all the people and things around you-and start being present with you and your inner life.

Rediscover, or maybe discover for the first time, who you are, what you stand for, what interests you, and what ignites a fire in your belly. What are those things that you are so passionate about that you can't stop

32

thinking about them? Then go do more of that, more of those things. Stop obsessing over your outer life—all the people and things around you—and start being present with you and your inner life.

Here's my list, short and simple. I'm not talking earth-shattering, groundbreaking, unheard of, lavish things, friends. I am talking about day-to-day simple joys and pleasures. Fill your cup first for once. Here are some ways I fill mine:

- Diffuse essential oils for the season or mood I'm in.
- Burn incense. This reminds me of yoga and church.
- Play music that fits my mood. Meditation to wake up and get going or during my prayer time, contemporary Christian when cooking or driving, and country when hanging outside around our fire pit.
- Treat myself to fun beverages. Hot tea while I read at night, coffee during my contemplative morning time, a refreshing cold beer with my pizza or while I'm at happy hour socializing with my coworkers, and a nice glass of red wine when enjoying a dinner date with my husband.
- Yoga as much as possible.
- Get outside for a walk and breathe in the fresh air
- Wake up early to spend quiet time with God through prayer and devotion.

As I started to recognize little things that brought me great joy, the things that kept me from embracing presence and from allowing myself to sink into these acts of self-love became glaringly apparent. See if any of these encroach on your personal space, eat away at joy in your life, or monopolize too much of your time:

- Negative thoughts, catastrophizing the future
- Calendars
- Worry over everyday happenings
- Thinking, worrying, and obsessing over what others think about me

When you find the courage—when you dig deep into your bellies and pull up the bravery that lies within you—you will see how saying "no" feels good. It feels right. And it will set you free. In his book *The Power of Now,* spiritual teacher and author Eckhart Tolle states, "When you say 'no' to a person or a situation, let it come not from reaction but from insight, from a clear realization of what is right or not right for you at that moment. Let it be a nonreactive 'no,' a high-quality 'no,' a 'no' that is free of all negativity, and so creates no further suffering." [3] We were never meant to be "yes" machines, friends. We have limits. We have needs. When we say no, we free ourselves to work on things we value, not what other people deem important. And, by saying no, we can more clearly hear what God is pressing on our hearts to say yes to. Say no to what doesn't matter to you (or God), so you can say yes to what does.

> **Say no to what doesn't matter to you (or God), so you can say yes to what does.**

Scripture

Matthew 5:37 *"All you need to say is simply 'Yes' or 'No'; anything beyond this comes from the evil one."*

Matthew 11:28-30 *"Come to me, all you who are weary and burdened, and I will give you rest. Take my yoke upon you and learn from me, for I am gentle and humble in heart, and you will find rest for your souls. For my yoke is easy, and my burden is light."*

Reflection

Make a list of your most recent "yeses." Are there things on this list that you wish you would have said "no" to? How can you free yourself of the need to constantly be the "yes" person? How will saying "no" affect you, your friendships, your career, and/or your family? What freedoms do you think you will find by saying yes less and more no?

_____

_____

_____

_____

Prayer

Dear God,

Thank you that your yoke is easy and your burden is light. Thank you that you promise to give us—the worried, hurried, pressured, and stressed—rest and peace for our souls if we'll just come before you. Thank you for knowing our concerns, for walking with us, and for helping us carry our burdens so we don't have to carry them alone. Forgive us for the times that we've tried to fix things in our own power, for not taking time to rest, or for coming to you first with our burdens. Help us to notice others who seem weary and burdened too, and give us the tools to help lessen their load by pointing them to you.

Chapter 3: Less Self-Sufficient, More Dependent

As human beings, we are wired to depend on each other. God created us to live in community, to learn from each other, and to guide and support one another.

I hate—or I used to hate—the feeling of being weak or needing help. I didn't like to be bad at new things—I'm still working on this. I certainly didn't ever let down my guard to show my weakness or lack of knowledge in any area of my daily life—except with my husband—I have always asked him for help. I have always wanted to be great at things—all the things. And if I felt I wasn't, I avoided them. It was that simple. And, since you're reading this, I'm going to lay money that you have often felt or do feel the same way. Fair enough. That's easy to understand since we live in a society that makes us feel being dependent is equal to being a "needy" failure. Dependence is often paired with words such as weak, helpless, clinging, incapable, and inferior. Who, may I ask, willingly wants to feel this way?

But what if we reframe our thinking around dependence? What if we view our dependence on others as a way of opening up, being seen, known, cared for, and loved—for all of who we are? Being dependent allows us to be vulnerable. Dependency actually forces vulnerability upon us. Relying on others requires we share our hearts and souls through meaningful, heartfelt connection. Being dependent is an act of truth-

> **Being dependent is an act of truth-telling. We are being genuine when we let others see and know that we can't do everything alone.**

telling. We are being genuine when we let others see and know that we can't do everything alone. This can be a gift to relationships because when people rely and count on each other for support and love, both feel respected, needed, valued, and loved. Being dependent in a healthy way produces relationships with mutual give and take, support, and encouragement. And people are happier to help than you think. I mean, when was the last time you helped someone in need, and it didn't feel your heart and happy meter? As human beings, we are wired to depend on each other. God created us to live in community, to learn from each other, and to guide and support one another. Finding your group– your community– will give you a strong sense of self. So you see, being dependent on others can be the strong foundation for enjoying independence in certain areas of our lives.

While we need to establish, tend to, and strengthen our personal communities—family, neighborhood, workplace, and church—we also need to tend to our inner spiritual connections. We serve and love a God that wants nothing more than for us to lean on, rely on, and trust in Him. The greatest form of reliance, need, and dependence

> **The greatest form of reliance, need and dependence that we will ever have in our earthly life is a deep dependence on God.**

that we will ever have in our earthly life is a deep dependence on God. Being dependent on God takes the benefit factor to a whole other level. God knows everything we're going through, and He knows best how to love us through it. He knows the best possible outcome. He knows all the bumps, curves, and detours ahead, so we need to rely on and depend on Him and trust Him with it all. He knows better than we do—so dependence on God is essential.

It's a trap that many of us fall into time and again. We believe we need to be great in order to be worthy, or we need to be interesting in order to be liked. We play this game of "I need to perform and show how amazingly awesome I am, and I can handle all the things all the time" to prove to people that we're worth being with. We take pride in wearing the "I never need help" badge of honor when what we really need is to be giving ourselves grace and model real vulnerability and courage by asking for help. After all, asking for help is indeed one of the bravest things we can do. I'm not going to lie. This is hard. For whatever reason—societal pressures, social norms, the in-your-face living, I have done it all and done it better mindset—we feel like we have to be self-sufficient. My story and my decision to share it openly and honestly with you is to tell you that it's okay to need help; it's smart to ask for it. Asking for help forces us into living a more surrendered life. We are releasing our grip, relinquishing our control, and allowing others to fill our space to meet our needs. Why walk around pretending not to need help, to not need anything from anybody? When we do that, when we choose to live our lives in that way, we're all faking that we're fine. Whom do we think we impress walking around with these superpower vibes in all walks and roles of our lives? We pretend to be another real or imagined person instead of being ourselves—our human selves—that need and, deep down in the depths of our souls, want help.

It was once said, "A comfort zone is a beautiful place, but nothing ever grows there." I am not sure who coined those words, but I do know that it is one of the truest things I have ever heard. Unfortunately for me, and something tells me for you too, my dear reader, self-sufficiency becomes our comfort zone. I know I would rather put my head down, furrow my brow, clench my jaws, and shoulder-hunch my way through my days than appear to need help or, heaven forbid, ask for it. I felt asking for help was a sign of weakness. Remember, I didn't like the feeling of being weak or needing help, so nose to the grindstone it was for me. At home, at work, in social situations, any and all settings, I was on stage. I was in performance and impress mode. If I dared felt less than, not equipped for, or in need of help, along with that came the feeling of shame. I was constantly living in a state of shame. And if you haven't been on it, the shame cycle is an easy place to get stuck. It's far easier than being vulnerable and asking for help. Just like I didn't like not being good at things, and I avoided trying new things for fear of failure, I did like staying in my comfort zone of shame. It was far more comforting to me to put off my independent, self-sufficient air rather than rely on, depend on, or show how much I needed others. I was so busy and working so hard to appear to have it all together all the time that I didn't have the clarity to see how much I did indeed need help or the energy to stop and take the time to get better.

I never really saw this self-sufficiency, "I am woman, hear me roar" mentality in myself until I tried to silently, self-sufficiently battle my way through my struggle with relentless insomnia. Which, in turn, marched me right into full-blown anxiety that dropped me into the depths and despair of depression. Remember, it was the summer, and for all intents and purposes, I should have been experiencing my refreshing inhale of relaxing days ahead as I exhaustedly exhaled the weariness from teaching another school year. But I was not relaxed at all.

As I opened up to Matt, shared with our parents and a few of my close friends, and tried to find a good counselor, I realized that I needed help. I could not face this dark, treacherous valley on my own. Pride and self-sufficiency had kept me from asking for help in the past- which I believe is fully responsible for how I ended up in this place anyway. And by not asking for help all those years and hiding my suffering due to shame through this storm, I had and was stunting my own growth. My intellectual growth, my emotional growth, my relational growth, and mostly my spiritual growth were all suffering.

Because I lived most of my life wanting to please others and put on a performance because I wanted to be special and significant, to make a mark on the world, I wanted to control and manipulate the growth of

> **But the battle God placed me in, the battle of my mind, showed me full stop that He designed me to need Him. My needs and His provisions are a perfect fit.**

my life. I would seek God and give matters to Him, but I always found myself quickly taking them back, "I've got this, God; I can handle this on my own." But the battle God placed me in, the battle of my mind, showed me full stop that He designed me to need Him. My needs and His provisions are a perfect fit. He gives us longings, feelings of incompleteness, and struggles as a way to remind us of our need for Him. God does not want us to bury or deny our feelings. Classic me would take those feelings and stuff them deep down and away or, even worse, ignore them altogether. God wants us to come to Him, to lay our burdens and worries down—lay it all at His feet. When we recognize, admit, and honor our reliance on Him, it helps us feel more intimate with Him. I learned that by drawing closer to God, He also drew me closer to my people. He softened my heart. He gently guided me to peaceful surrender, and I allowed others in to help me, to love me, to hold me.

If you've never read, listened to, or watched any of Kate Bowler's works, I highly recommend that you do! You won't be sorry; I promise. Bowler is unabashedly bashing the toxic positivity that is our culture. She has, and still is, weathering a horrific storm in her own life, and she often talks about the fact that loneliness is a public health crisis and disconnection affects our ability to weather life's most difficult storms. Life is hard. We all carry our own share of pain, heartache, and disappointments, so why pretend as if we don't? Why pretend we're fine? Why pretend we're living the dream? When the truth is we're not fine, we could be better, and we're living through nightmares? I have learned that part of living well is learning to suffer well. I used to hide away the idea of a bad day, and now I treasure how I let myself feel those feelings and ride the wave. True living is learning to let ourselves be sad, grieve, cry, and pay attention to our aches. I now see that when I recognize and care for the tender parts in my soul, those dark, scary, unwanted places of anxiety, depression, and loneliness, I feel less alone, and they are finally seen. And so am I. As we open up and accept what we are really feeling, we become more united with ourselves and with God. We can release a little, untighten our grip, and let go of our breath. We can relinquish the desire to fix, ignore, change, stuff down, or numb out. We can finally feel. We all have things that we have to suffer in this life, but we don't have to suffer the extra burden and heaviness that comes from denying, hiding, or shaming our pain away. Once we make this connection to ourselves, we can ask those closest to us, the safe, loved ones that God has placed in our lives to ride the wave with us, providing us some comfort and relief.

My connections, once I opened up to them, let them in, and let them help me, literally saved me. But, I had to release my prideful badge of honor, I had to share my weaknesses and my fears, and I had to trust others with my life. The first person I turned to was, of course, Matt, my husband. I knew I had been suffering for some time. He knew I was getting next to zero sleep, and he knew I was anxious and feeling down, but he didn't know how very scared I was. He didn't know I was at the end of my rope and about to let go. So when I came completely clean about how dark, scary, and intrusive my thoughts had become, he vowed to stand by my side and help me get the help I needed. I remember Matt holding my face in his hands, his tear-filled eyes looking into mine also full of tears, and he said, "I don't know how to help you. I can't fix this. But I will be by your side every step you take." And by my side, he was. He drove me to my first counseling in-take session, he made the call to set up the first appointment with my psychiatrist, he held my trembling hands when we sat on our bed with our kids, then ages 14, 12, 10, and 8, and I tried my best to explain to them what was happening with me. And, most importantly, he prayed for me, he prayed over me, he prayed with me. We both knew in the depths of our hearts and minds that God had us every step of the way, and we were relentless in storming his gates in prayer on behalf of my health. Boy, were we scared…but God.

Things were changing for me. I was in a position where I could no longer function as I had before. I had to take time off work. I knew I needed to, but I couldn't bring myself to admit it. I will be forever grateful for my supportive, caring principal at the time, who told me to take two weeks off from work to rest and care for myself. She told me to walk away, not to even give work another thought. And she made sure that happened. She made calls, secured my time off, arranged for substitutes, and made sure the other parts of my job were tended to. This was a colossal step for me. I never wanted my coworkers to view me as someone who needed help. After all, I was the helper, the doer, but my anxiety and depression had left me with less–less energy, less clarity, less focus, less to give, and less to offer. I just couldn't go on. It took me months to realize that just because I was doing less, being less, pouring out less, and giving less, it didn't make me less. It allowed my coworkers of twenty years to see that I was human, something I had masked with all my superhuman efforts. For once, I was giving to myself. I was filling myself. And honestly, looking back, allowing them to see me in this state–a state of needing help, asking for help, and taking help gave me so much freedom, and it showed them that I wasn't as invincible as I pretended to be. I now live with the freedom of knowing my limits, accepting and appreciating the limits of others, and being okay with just enough for today, no more, no less. I know now that God was waiting patiently all those years for me to ask Him

> I know now that God was waiting patiently all those years for me to ask Him for help.

for help. And He freely gifted me with family, friends, and coworkers to be the ones that would come along to help me and love me.

What I learned through this eye-opening, life-changing experience of letting others in, showing my true colors, and putting down my guard is that embracing my tenderness and vulnerability is just as important, probably more so, than having all the answers, doing all the things, pleasing everybody, and always being the helper but never asking for help. I learned we "Helpers" need help too. Before I opened my heart and let myself depend on others, I wasn't a very compassionate person. I was a no-nonsense, do your job and do it right, and stop complaining kind of gal. My first response was to judge others' lack of performance and perfection. I would self-protect by pointing out others' flaws, or I would dive head-first into fix-it mode. I became much more vulnerable when I started seeing a counselor. At that point in my journey, I had not yet publicly shared my story. Those closest to me knew why I was taking time off work, and my family was in the fire with me. They were all loving me through my day-to-day struggles. Going to talk to a stranger about what I was going through, sharing the intimacies of my struggle, the feelings of darkness and despair, the reality that I had times where I felt harming myself or being gone altogether would be better than what I was putting Matt and the kids through, was a colossal effort for me. It was frightening. Opening up for the first time in my life about where, why, and how I felt weak, worthless, or non-useful with a stranger was mortifying to me. I was the one that scoffed at others for needing to take medicine to feel good. I was one of the first to pass judgment on someone "needing to talk to someone about your problems." You're a big girl; figure it out yourself was my motto. That is until I met my counselor.

I was scared to death to walk into her office on the day of my first visit, but I was also desperate for help, any kind of help from anyone. I was shaming myself the whole way there. I had to drive past the kids' schools to get to her office, and I remember thinking, "What is wrong with you, Jodi? Matt and the kids are at work and school, going about their days and getting things done, living life. And here you are, home from work, crying through your days, and driving to counseling because you need help pulling it together!?!" I also remember the night before going to counseling. I felt so hopeless and weak that I needed a counselor. But seeking counseling opened the door to my vulnerability—it opened me up to others and to myself. To have the perspective of my counselor, someone who was deeply rooted in self-compassion and willing to embrace my struggles without judging me or offering up quick "fix it" advice and pointing out my strengths that I had swept under the rug, was refreshing. She simply shared her perception, her insights on what I was going through, and my reaction to it. She questioned me so that I would reflect on my own actions. Why do I do that thing? Why did I say those words? My need to talk about the same feeling, the same fear, the same shame over and over was exhausting for Matt. He would never admit that, but I know it was—it had to be. He was worried about me. He was worried about the kids. He wanted to help me. He wanted to help us. He's like me in that regard, but he knew he couldn't. My experience was too personal for him to be able to give an outside, fresh perspective. He was hurting right along with me.

> He used this time of tribulation to teach me that I need Him, and I need the people He has placed in my life. We are made for community.

Opening my heart and shifting my mindset to accepting the fact that dependency is the way to go has changed me forever. God was trying to teach me this all along, and I just kept ignoring Him. People have offered to help me in big and small ways numerous times in my life, and I just always said, "Nah, I got it." Well, God brought me to my knees, so the only way I could look was up. He used this time of tribulation to teach me that I need Him, and I need the people He has placed in my life. We are made for community. 1 Corinthians 12:26-27 says, "If one part suffers, every part suffers with it; if one part is honored, every part rejoices with it. Now you are the body of Christ, and each one of you is a part of it," We were literally created to be a part of one another's lives—the mountaintop highs and the dark valleys. He gave us each other! Why could I not have realized the importance of that sooner? I thought I was doing everyone around me a favor by not being "needy" and by being the friend and family member who always helped but never asked for or needed help herself. But then it dawned on me: I love helping my family and friends. It gives me joy, and I count it an honor to be other people's go-to person. It is a gift to have each other. It is also a gift to need each other.

We never outgrow our parents, and this certainly was a time in my life that I needed mine. And they were there—every step of the way. When I first let Mom and Dad know I was going to take some time off work to rest and heal, they asked if I wanted them to come be with me, Matt, and the kids. I initially told them 'no'; I was okay and just needed some time. Well, it wasn't even two days later, I found myself picking up the phone with trembling hands and tears streaming down my face, asking them to come be with me. Without hesitation, they threw some clothes in a bag, hopped in their car, and were at my door in a matter of hours. Mom and Dad didn't come to fix me or attempt to make everything better. They didn't ask a lot of questions, they didn't tell me there was nothing to worry or be anxious about, and they didn't try to take matters into their own parent problem-solving hands. They were just there–present and loving on me the way they always had. They took walks with me, they sat outside and talked with me, they prayed over me, and they assured me they would help see me through this time. I've already shared how tenderly my dad loved me through this storm, and the same holds true with my mom. I'll never forget a tender moment between the two of us, a moment where she reminded me that I was her baby. A moment when she held my hands as I lay in my bed crying, and she prayed over me and told me she would take the best care of me that she could. It was the night before I was going to be admitted to the hospital to have my second heart ablation—my first ablation was a few years prior, and for lack of a better word, it was unsuccessful. At this point in time, I had been battling my lack of sleep and anxiety for a few months, and I desperately wanted the heart ablation to fix it all—make it all better. And, deep down, that's what Mom wanted too. We all did. We figured I was anxious about my heart "acting up" again. Once the procedure was over—this time hopefully with success—we were all assuming I would be less anxious, finding myself able to sleep again and returning to my old self. Mom knelt next to my bed that night and, through teary eyes, said, "I think once you get through this procedure, you're going to feel much better." I, knowing deep in my gut that what I was experiencing was not just my heart "acting up," cried back to her, "But what if it's not my heart? What if I don't feel better?" In the way only a fierce, loving mom can do, she quickly replied, "Well, then we'll cross that bridge next. We're going to do this together one day at a time, one step at a time."

Just as we never outgrow our parents, this season in my life showed me that we need our kids just as much as they need us. They can teach us just as much, if not more, as we teach them if we have our hearts and minds open to see and learn from them. My kids, along with my husband, loved me fiercely through my storm. I hated that they saw me anxious and depressed. I worried that I would cause them to feel this way too. I was embarrassed and felt worthless when they would head off to school and see that I wasn't going to work. But, I learned through a lot of counseling, a lot of talking, a lot of sharing, and a lot of listening that I was actually setting a strong example for my kids. I was showing them what it meant to be brave. I was asking for help and getting help–they saw, first-hand, that it is indeed okay to ask for help. My months of struggle were such transformative years for them, especially for Anna and Jack. And my worry over how they were dealing with my situation—how they were coping and responding—just added to my already heap of existing anxiety. But those kids, they rallied around me and supported my journey.

Anna joined me on the couch one night after we got home from a church Christmas show. She wrapped her arms around me, laid her head on my shoulder, and whispered, "I know you're working so hard to get better, Mom. I feel like you're doing better, do you? It made my heart happy to see you smiling and singing in church tonight." Gosh! That meant the world to me. She saw me. She knew I was working, trying. I wasn't going to give up on my family or myself. She knew that I loved her and was doing everything in my power to feel good again. And she noticed that I was reaching for God, clinging to Him to carry me through.

Another example of the fierce love that shined out of my kiddos came from Maggie. She was in third grade when I was going through this tumultuous time, and she was sick one day and needed to stay home from school with me. I had my first appointment with the psychologist scheduled for that day, and I was worried about taking her with me. What would she think? What would she say? What would she ask? But I was out of options. Keeping her at home and taking her with me was how it had to be. I will never in all my life forget what happened when we pulled into the parking lot of the doctor's office. Since she wasn't feeling well, I walked around to Maggie's side of the van to open her door and help her get out of her booster seat (she was tiny, so yes, she was still in a booster seat!). She said, "Mommy, I have something for you. Close your eyes." I was perplexed as to what she may have to give me, but I closed my eyes and stuck my hand out, eager to find out. I felt her little hand place a smooth, round, heavy-ish object in my hand. Maggie then chirped, "Okay, Mommy, open your eyes for my surprise!" Reader, grab your tissues. Because when I tell you what I saw laying, ever so lovingly, in my hand, you're going to cry, no doubt. I looked down and saw the most beautiful, bright pink rock lying in the palm of my hand. It was speckled with white dots, and in bold black lettering, it told me, "Love the way you are." Friend, that slayed me. I was done. I burst into tears, grabbed Maggie in my arms, and squeezed her so tight. She started giggling, "Mommy, let me go—that tickles me." I put her down, grabbed her hand, and briskly started walking into the doctor's office, not wanting to be late for my appointment. As we walked in, I looked down at Maggie and told her how much the rock meant to me and how happy it made my heart. She said, "Mommy, I love you just the way you are, and I know you are going to feel better soon."

The kids were constantly checking on me, asking me how I was feeling, telling me they loved me, and coming up to hug and kiss me. Abby, while only in fifth grade at the time, would always ask me about

> **I wanted to normalize going to a counselor; I wanted my kids to view my counseling sessions just as they viewed their well checkups with the pediatrician.**

my sessions with my counselor. I had explained to her why I was going to counseling and how it helped me. I wanted to normalize going to a counselor; I wanted my kids to view my counseling sessions just as they viewed their well checkups with the pediatrician. So when I would return from a session with my counselor, Abby was always the first to ask, "What did you learn today, Mommy?" Another sweet act that touched my heart was I would find little notes all over the house encouraging me to keep going and keep doing the work to get and feel better. But the first day I returned to work, the notes were next level. Each of my kids had personally written me a note letting me know they believed in me, they knew I was going to be successful with going back to work, that my students would be excited to see me, and that they wouldn't know what they would do without me. I vividly remember Jack's note. He was in 7th grade at the time, so I know writing notes to his mom was not something that came naturally. But he did, and it meant the world to me. I actually found Jack's note in my desk drawer just the other day when I was cleaning it out for the end of the year. As a lump formed in my throat, I gazed at his note through blurred, teary eyes. In his precise, near perfect penmanship I read the words Jack wrote more than 5 years ago, "I love you! You do so much for us, and we are so proud to call you Mom!" It still does my momma heart good to read these words. My kids were and are proud of me, and that feels amazing. My kids have told me that in watching me go through my difficult time, they learned how to be brave. They learned how to ask for help and how to let others help them. They let me know they saw that I was hurting, and they saw that I was getting help. My kids saw me fall down–hard–but they also saw me get back up.

Our culture values independence. The "I am woman, hear me roar!" mantra has never been shouted louder than it is today. Well, God has a different way, a better way. That was the one and only thing that was wrong with Creation—man will not be alone. He created us to be together. Letting people in to be a part of our lives can be scary. It's hard to let people into our suffering. It's hard to admit we can't handle the pain. It's so much easier to let them into our rejoicing and success. But suffering and rejoicing are intertwined; they are both a part of the human experience. Our successes are by the grace of God, and only God can heal our suffering.

> **Our successes are by the grace of God, and only God can heal our suffering.**

While my time away from work afforded me the opportunity to seek the help I needed, it was one of the most arduous, frightening things I have ever faced. But in that time, I felt so loved– not just loving, but wrapped in other people's love. It was no more striving. I had come to a place where I was laying it all down. Even though I was so overwhelmed and so scared during the weekdays when I was home alone, I also had an unexplainable peace about me. The unimaginable, the unthinkable, felt manageable. I felt terrible some days and other days were very heavy, but through it all, I still felt loved. I felt held. God's presence, his reign supreme, covered me, protected me, and carried me through it all.

When I was home alone, day after day, my dependence on God and my trust and faith in Him grew like no other time before in my life. All I had was time–time to talk with God, time to cry out to Him in desperation, time to yell at Him out of anger and frustration, time to read the Bible, time to pray, walk, think, reflect, and listen to what He was trying to say to me. It was a true transformation. Since that time, five years ago, my faith has remained supremely solid. I spend time in God's Word every day. I pray all throughout my days, not just when I need something. I talk about my relationship with Jesus more openly than ever before. I share the importance of mental and spiritual well-being. God is an integral part of my everyday life, not just someone I visit at church every Sunday. What we need and what he provides fit together perfectly.

He never meant for us to be self-sufficient. In fact, He designed us to need Him not just for the little, day-to-day things but for all the things great and small. He doesn't want us to bury our feelings of want and need; He planted those in us so we would need Him and rely on Him. He asks us to come to him with all our neediness and with our defenses down. He longs for us to be made complete in Him. And I was. I am. And so, too, are you. He is more than enough. He is all we have ever needed and all we will ever need. His grace is sufficient for us, so let's depend on Him alone.

In my unlearning of the absurd way of thought that self-sufficiency is the only way to live, I learned I don't always have to be strong. It's okay to be sad and to be supported. It's okay to need help, and it's brave to ask for it. My breakdown gave me permission to be imperfect, and now I don't fear imperfection; I embrace it. I carry no shame over who I am, what I say, what I do, or, more importantly, what I DON'T do! After I walked through the most fiery parts of the storm or allowed God to carry me, I became more comfortable with sharing my struggles with others. It opened the doors for me to hear others' stories or for them to start sharing their own story. When we share our stories of struggle and when we ask for help, we are building a bridge of connection with others, possible nonbelievers, that is far stronger than the bridge our "perfect lives" portrayed could ever build. Sharing our brokenness will shine the light and love of Jesus far better than our pretend wholeness ever could. When we earn the trust of others by sharing our true, whole, broken selves, we will earn each other's trust and our own vulnerability. When we break, that's where God's light pours in. As Christians, we aren't doing anyone any favors by pretending that all we do is win when we follow and have a relationship with Jesus. It is better to share our true, authentic, flawed selves because that's what really reveals God's goodness, mercy,

> **Sharing our brokenness will shine the light and love of Jesus far better than our pretend wholeness ever could.**

> **If others can see God's presence, His goodness, in the middle of our messes, then they may just come to notice Him in the middle of their messes too.**

compassion, and grace. When I began sharing about my anxiety and depression, my going to counseling, my need for medication, and my time off work, I shared how I, too, am still learning to find God and depend on Him in the middle of life's toughest battles. If others can see God's presence, His goodness, in the middle of our messes, then they may just come to notice him in the middle of their messes too.

Scripture

2 Corinthians 12:9 *"But he said to me, 'My grace is sufficient for you, for my power is made perfect in weakness.' Therefore I will boast all the more gladly about my weaknesses so that Christ's power may rest on me."*

Reflection

Think of a time when you didn't ask for help, but you really needed it. How would that time look differently if you had asked for help? Would the outcomes, or your mindset during the process, have been more positive if you had reached out for help? List three people in your life you know you can always count on to help you when you need it. Who is someone in your life that you can help, and how specifically can you help them? Do they know you are willing to be their support and help person?

Reflect on a time when you were struggling your way through an area of weakness. How were God's strength and power evident during that time? How can you point others to Jesus' saving grace by sharing your weaknesses and stories of struggle?

_____

_____

_____

_____

Prayer

Dear Lord,

Thank you for placing people in my life that I know can and will help me anytime I need them. Deliver me from this illusion that I am self-sufficient. Grant me the grace to accept my limits and turn to others, and You, more regularly. Give me the willingness to let friends and family be a part of my struggles and support me in carrying my burdens and worries. Give me a mind and heart that sees and knows that I, in and of myself, am not enough. I need to turn to you and know that your grace is sufficient for me.

Chapter 4: Less Striving, More Thriving

God needed to teach me that the world will never be fully satisfied with me, and neither will I. But He is. He always has been, and He always will be.

After a long, physically, and mentally exhausting day, I found my brain telling my finger to swipe up over and over again. In an attempt to numb out, I was mindlessly scrolling through Instagram when it hit me. "You are afraid of surrender because you don't want to lose control, but you never had control. All you had was anxiety." This post by the amazingly gifted writer Elizabeth Gilbert grabbed my attention. I had not stopped to consume or process a post in the last 30 minutes of my numbing out, but this stopped me dead in my tracks. Was she really telling me that all my striving, perfecting, performing, controlling, and managing tactics were not me being in control but rather were signs of me living with anxiety? I did stop and consume this; I even read the well-versed explanation in the caption, and I found myself reading, reflecting, and responding in the comment section.

That was it. That was my life, my personality, my way of being–neatly wrapped and tied with a bow. I thought to myself, "Jodi, you don't have control of all the people and all the things. You have anxiety." And living in this constant state of striving can be, and was for me, very dangerous. I was constantly striving and not taking the time to enjoy happiness over reaching my goals. I was looking for faster, better, and prettier rather than allowing myself to feel confidence and joy. It took me a long time to realize that I would never, could never, attain perfection. There will always be something I can strive for. Always. My self-imposed goals (or burdens, rather) became deeply personal. I judged my self-worth on whether or not my performance toward my goals was good enough. This led to a continuous state of stress. I was always striving to be better. I never had moments where I reached the point of satisfaction. There was literally no rest, no break from my self-imposed stress. I felt the need and pressure to work and perform at all times. My self-imposed, high- stake, high-standard, perfect, or else, way of living inevitably led to me feeling like I was in failure mode most of the time, which walked me into burnout, anxiety, and depression.

For the majority of my forty-six years, I bought into this mantra—the mantra of do, do, DO! Strive, Strive, Strive! I told myself, "The more you do, Jodi, the more people will see you, hear you, praise you, look up to you, and strive to be you." I come from a family of doers. And I am madly in love with these people; they are the hardest working, most integrity-filled people you will ever meet. Not only do they put in the hard work at their jobs, but they pour hard work into their families, into their friendships, and most importantly, into their relationships with Jesus. I was taught to work hard at doing whatever needed to be done. Whether that was to get good grades, to make the sports team, or to get whatever achievement, award, or recognition I was seeking. If I was going to set goals, I was going to work hard to achieve them. I was taught to work hard at doing—doing good for myself, doing good for my family, and doing good for others. The worth that I attached to the outcome of my work, that was on me. My parents, my family, and my friends didn't love me less or feel differently about me if I didn't succeed. They never once made me feel less than. I did that all on my own.

Growing up, I absorbed the idea that hard work is good work, and it is, my friend, it really, truly is. There is not one single negative attribute that can be given to hard work. And, for most of my life, this intense desire to do, do, do served me very well. High school and college consisted of friends, social activities, getting good grades, making the cheer and track teams, being a part of honor societies, student councils, graduating with honors, getting a master's degree during my first year of teaching, becoming a nationally board certified and master teacher, and on, and on, and on…

I would be serving up a colossal dose of ingratitude if I didn't hit the pause button here and make it crystal clear that I love, respect, admire and adore my parents, my brother, and my extended and current immediate family as well as my closest friends. The identity and blessing of being a member of this amazing group of DOers have served me very well. Much of what I have today is due to the life lessons these amazing people taught, modeled, mentored, and rallied around me to do. They have driven, inspired, and motivated me to do more, to be better, and to work harder. I have just always found myself surrounded by people that, for lack of better terms, get s#*! done. And, as I said, I love them for this, and I love myself for all of the accomplishments and recognition I have had in this life. BUT…

When did the accomplishments become more important than the hard work itself? When did the accolades begin holding higher value than the actual effort of just showing up and trying?

Look at that last statement… "I love myself for all of the accomplishments…" What?! When did the accomplishments become more important than the hard work itself? When did the accolades begin holding higher value than the actual effort of just showing up and trying?

They didn't. At least not in the eyes of my parents, my brother, my husband, my family, and my friends. I did. I made the accolades, recognitions, and the list of numerous calendar events the goal—not the hard work, not the trying, or the showing up. As a working mom of four, I have been torn between being able to do it all as any good mother does and doing it all for my students as any good teacher does. For a sampling of my madness, I will share with you that, in addition to the incessant "need" to cook a full meal, get the laundry and grocery shopping done mid-week, because who wants to do that garbage on the weekends (insert, who has time? We have eight games, practices, social events to be at)? I coached, joined committees, signed up to help in my kids' classrooms by doing tasks from home at night because I couldn't be in their classrooms during the day–I was running my own classroom. I signed up to bring in food for their teachers, used my personal days to go to their classrooms and read or chaperone a field trip, gave more than the mandatory "parent help hours" for plays, taught Vacation Bible School, volunteered in the church nursery, or whatever it is that was happening at the time. All of this and more, and I would still feel it necessary to be early to work, early to meetings, have the perfect paperwork, bring work home every single night, and sometimes lose time and presence with my kids because I "needed" to do school work. You see the predicament here; when at work, I felt guilty about not being with my kids; and when I was at home, I would be distracted by my work performance. I always felt that I wasn't *DOING* enough in any of the places for any of the people. But I figured if I *DID* enough, that would be enough. So, I was the mom of four and a teacher that felt the more I signed up for, the better I would feel, and the more people would acknowledge me, praise me, and maybe even envy me. Wow! Look at her! She does it all, and she does it all so well!

Wrong. So wrong in every single way imaginable! Why? Because I missed out on so much. While I was busy riding the express train, doing all of the things, in all of the places, for all of the people, I

> **While I was busy riding the express train, doing all of the things, in all of the places, for all of the peple, I lost a sense of BEing.**

lost a sense of BEing. I could not be further from thriving. One day I started to realize that in all the doing, I was missing it, all of it. The days became a big blur of getting up just to do, do, do! And at the end of each day, I found I couldn't remember what I had actually done. Sure, I had big, red check marks next to all of my "to do" items for the day, but did I do anything that really mattered, anything that resembled living and being? Did I have a meaningful conversation with someone? Probably not, because my mind was five steps ahead on my next thing to do. Did I have things I was grateful for at the end of each day? Not really; I was too mentally and physically exhausted to serve up thanks for much of anything. Did I look into my babies' eyes when they talked to me and listen, really listen? Nope. I was too busy whipping up dinner, doing laundry, and checking work email. I was addicted to work. I worked at work, I worked at home, I worked at church, and I worked in the kids' activities. Looking back, I now realize my health suffered—both physically and mentally. I did not, at the time, require intervention. I just kept my nose to the grindstone and powered through. I thrived on the "Great job!" affirmations and the "How would we do this without you?" praises. My productivity and busyness gave me a sense of value and self-worth. All the to-dos made me feel needed and valued.

> **He needed to teach me that the world will never be fully satisfied with me, and neither will I. But God is. He always has been, and He always will be. I am complete in His eyes. And so are you.**

Getting free from this deadly cycle meant going through a season of struggle so God could teach me. He needed to teach me that the world will never be fully satisfied with me, and neither will I. But God is. He always has been, and He always will be. I am complete in His eyes. And so are you.

This cycle of doing lasted way too long, and it took a monstrous wake-up call from the Man Upstairs to get me off the hamster wheel. I was literally running in circles but making no progress with things that really mattered. I was doing things the same way, repeating the same mistakes. I was guided by a sense that motion, doing, is the important thing. I just needed to keep going. Until God made me realize I didn't.

He put a full press, hard stop on the madness. Getting free from this deadly cycle meant going through a season of struggle so God could teach me. It was time off work, doctor visits, trials with various medications, hundreds of hours of counseling, more time in His word, and more time talking with Him. And listening to Him! He loved me hard through this battle. He kept my eyes above the water, and He graciously showed me how my significance had been misplaced in my doing rather than my being. I was driven by the to-dos; my identity and purpose were entrenched in impressing others, pleasing others, proving myself, and producing with perfection. During this forced pause in my life, He showed me that I didn't know who I really was. I thought I was just a perfectionist, high-performing type of person. But what I have learned and come to realize is that which Brene Brown speaks to in her book *The Gifts Of Imperfection,* "Where perfectionism exists, shame is always lurking. In fact, shame is the birthplace of perfectionism." Brown goes on to explain. "Perfectionism is not the same thing as striving to be your best. Perfectionism is not about healthy achievement and growth. Perfectionism is the belief that if we live perfect, look perfect, and act perfect, we can minimize or avoid the pain of blame, judgment, and shame. It's a shield. Perfectionism is not self-improvement. Perfectionism is, at its core, about trying to earn approval and acceptance. Somewhere along the way, we adopt this dangerous and debilitating belief system: I am what I accomplish and how well I accomplish it." Brown has written her own definition of perfectionism, where she describes it as "Perfectionism is self-destructive and addictive..." It is "an unattainable goal." And she says, "It is in the process of embracing our imperfections that we find our truest gifts: courage, compassion, and connection." [1]

I feared if I stopped and gave it all up, I wouldn't be worthy or valued. If I slowed my roll, everything would fall apart. But what I have come to realize

> But what I have come to realize is when I let go, when I ease up, when I stop striving and surviving, I can finally fully rest and thrive in whom I need most, Jesus.

is when I let go, when I ease up, when I stop striving, I can finally fully rest and thrive in whom I need most, Jesus. Jesus will empower us to overcome what we're struggling with and regain our peace. It is clear to me that God used my insomnia to let me know something was awry. I was too busy to listen during the day, so when my body was still at night, this was what got my attention. So now I know God uses our bodies to talk to us—and we need to listen. I am still learning to listen to my body and what it is trying to tell me, what it wants me to know. I need to keep learning and growing in how to make proactive changes and better my way of living before my body shuts down and my heart breaks. I waited too long. I let months of insomnia and anxiety riddle me and tear me apart before I asked for help.

I love my bed, I love to sleep, and I need sleep. So when I didn't get adequate sleep for months on end, things went awry, and my existence got really ugly, real fast. My longing for my bed and a deep, rest-filled, peaceful sleep didn't always match up with my ability to get to sleep. In an effort to get one more thing crossed off my endless to-do list, I was working so frantically right up until, or more accurately, past my bedtime that I would collapse into bed eager and certain of sleep to come, and then it didn't. This was my mojo for years. Keep doing things until I could not do one more thing. Fall into bed, fast asleep for about three hours. Wake up—toss-and-turn, sweaty, anxiety-ridden awake until time for the alarm that signaled the start of another day on the hamster wheel of life. I would lie awake, riddled with worry and disappointment over not having finished everything that I set out to accomplish each day. I would ruminate over the fact that I hadn't done it all, which meant I felt like I hadn't done enough because it would still be waiting for me the next day. The problem with this is I couldn't surrender to the fact that I would not ever accomplish it all. Yesterday always carried over into tomorrow, and so every today felt heavy and full before it even started.

I had to fall hard to realize my genuine, God-given worth. I even put up a shield with my counselor. Not knowing her, nor having never met her before, I spent the first few sessions telling her everything I do. I mean everything. I wanted to impress her. I wanted her to admire me. I wanted her to say, "Wow! Jodi, you are something else!" As I cried through these sessions and apologized for crying (which I now know we should never do—we need to let ourselves feel the feelings), my counselor finally asked me around our third session, "Jodi, who are you? What do you like? What do you need? What do you do for yourself? What are your passions? What are your interests?" I struggled to answer her. She quickly pointed out to me that what I was and how I was defining myself was related to what I do for everyone else. My worth, my value, came from doing more for others, being a "Jack of all trades and master of none." I was labeling myself by what others thought of me. She told me I needed to just slow down and find myself: my faith, my worth, my identity, and my purpose for myself so that I can truly be seen, known, and loved by the important people in my life. I needed to let down the guards, lower the sword, and just be me—truly me!

My counselor at that time, helped me realize that I was suffering from anxiety. I mean, I have always been a type A, driven-by-a-motor kind of person, but I never thought of it as being anxiety. She helped me understand that I was suffering from over-functioning anxiety, which looks like doing everything for everyone, giving advice, taking on all of the responsibility, always helping, needing to be busy, and finding it hard to sit still. Yep, that was me. And she opened my eyes to see that I had hit a wall which caused me to shift to under-functioning anxiety: letting others do everything, asking for advice when you know what you need to do, avoiding responsibility, and always needing help. This was a huge one for me. I didn't even want Matt to leave the house; I was that scared. I felt paralyzed, and it was hard to get anything done. Yep, that was what happened to me.

Through God's grace and with the help of my insightful, thoughtful, caring, empathetic, yet honest counselor, I found my un-rootable, unshakeable purpose, a purpose that was not even close to the one I had been living. I realized my purpose was to find God, to love God, to listen to God, and to love the amazing humans he has blessed me with. Unlike the purpose of perfection, I had pressed myself to please and impress others. This journey with God took me from being a doer to actually being. He used a seemingly insurmountable challenge in my life to produce perseverance. In all honesty, a character trait that I was lacking. Because my life had been rather uneventful in a hard pressing way, and I was living the "life is good" slogan, I had not developed grit or perseverance. Two essential traits that He knew full well I would need, like a flower needs water, in the upcoming year. I began to understand that I was saying I was a woman of faith and that I was not defined by what I do but by who I am. But I was not truly living this. I was putting on a good show. People don't know you aren't handling and managing everything "perfectly" until you show them until you tell them. As well as being true to myself, I needed to be true to the people in my life. And, I realize now, why not be honest about it? We're all in this together. We need each other. We need grace from others, and we need to give grace in return. God gave it to me during this struggle; He always has, and He always will. Bottom line, I learned that God's purpose for me doesn't ever shift. That purpose is to surrender to Him, to serve Him, to love Him, to love His people, and to be at peace with Him. All the people—including myself. I needed to be worthy from the inside out. I needed to own my story to gain access to my worthiness—feeling I was enough, just as I was. It took a lot for me to stop striving to survive and to learn to be present, content, and thrive.

I have gone into brief detail about how God worked in painstaking ways to guide me, protect me, and love me through the greatest growth journey of my life. He made it crystal clear that life is not about everything I am doing but about how I do it. How I be. Not that I be everything to everybody, but that I be everything to the people who really matter. Him being at the top of the list. He says, "'Be still, and know that I am God" (Psalm 46:10). For anyone who may be struggling with anxiety, depression, or any other life battle, know that God will redeem your trial for His glory. Trust me, I know. I am sharing this story with you so that you may find comfort and hope in the hurting. I learned that only God can replenish what I had allowed the world to take from me. I know it's easier said than done to cease striving, to be still, and surrender our worries to Him. I would hand mine over and quickly take them back. I still do at times. It is an intentional, daily practice to carve out areas of my life where I am not striving. I have to plan times in my day when I do nothing and think of nothing. But if we want to truly thrive and enjoy life despite the many challenges we must lay down our desire to strive for, then we are merely existing.

So, what does this look like for me now? Well, I will be the first to admit that I am still a doer. I like to be busy. But, I have learned that I need to start every day by getting up before anyone else in the house so that I have quiet time. Just me and Jesus. In this time with Him, he has shown me that I don't have to be worried over every little thing. He lovingly speaks to me, "Therefore I tell you, do not worry about your life, what you will eat or drink; or about your body, what you will wear. Is not life more than food, and the body more than clothes? Look at the birds of the air; they do not sow or reap or store away in barns, and yet your heavenly Father feeds them. Are you not much more valuable than they? Can any one of you by worrying add a single hour to your life" (Matthew 6:25-27). I don't have to respond to every email; I don't have to sign up for everything under the sun; I don't have to cook a full meal every night of the week. Truth be told, my kids prefer it this way! I don't have to be the "Yes Woman" to all requests for help and volunteers. I can choose to say no to that social gathering in exchange for a quiet night at home. I can step aside and let others step up to fill the SignUp Genius slots. I can let the laundry pile up. (I mean, let's be real—it's not going anywhere! It can wait.) I can let the house be a smidge untidy and find the willpower to walk past those shoes, those coats, those

> I have finally come to the full realization that God does not need or want my charisma, my strength, or my accomplishments. He wants me.

clothes, that pile of stuff on the counter. I can leave it and let someone else get it—or not!

I have finally come to the full realization that God does not need or want my charisma, my strength, or my accomplishments. He wants me. He could not care less whether I have a successful platform with hundreds of thousands of followers, a book deal, or an impressive salary. He doesn't need me to perform in order for Him to stick around. He wants me just as I am. He wants me to come to Him when I'm tired, weary, and weak. He can do so much more than me. He can take my hard days, my broken days, my ordinary days and do some extraordinary things. He prefers our pitiful, repenting hearts over our stories of success. After all, we live in an upside-down kingdom, and our weaknesses are exactly what Jesus wants. He wants us to see the "closed-door" circumstances in our lives as His faithfulness instead of our failures. We must trust in His timing. It is far better to take our time and have things fall in place than to rush and have everything fall apart. Slow down. Stop striving. See how God will provide.

> He can take my hard days, my broken days, my ordinary days and do some extraordinary things. He prefers our pitiful, repenting hearts over the stories of success.

> He wants us to see the "closed-door" circumstances in our lives as His faithfulness instead of our failures.

If I had only realized how much living I was sacrificing by all my striving, I would take it all back in an instant. I was living under the false impression that I could control everything that happened in my life and the lives of my loved ones. But this is no way to live; it's so out of touch. There are circumstances that are beyond our control–a loved one dies, a friend gets a grim diagnosis, our spouse cheats or leaves, or we suffer the loss of a job–but we can control our response and our reaction to these

> We grow during the hard times-we resist them, yes, and we do everything we can to avoid them, but the hard is where the good is growing the best.

circumstances. And when I learned a more surrendered way of living, I was able to respond more reflectively, more responsibly. I was such a reactor. I was overreacting much of the time because I thought I had lost control, but again it was God's way of reminding me that the control was never really mine. Also, there is a lot of good that comes out of the bad, hard times. I have learned to embrace good suffering. We grow during the hard times—we resist them, yes, and we do everything we can to avoid them, but the hard is where the good is growing the best. And it's important that we allow ourselves to grow. I am so glad that I had no choice but to stop, learn, and grow from my season of struggle. This experience, this growth, changed me. It developed me. I am here writing this, and you are here reading this, so that means we've all made it through 100% of our most difficult days. I no longer survive my days. Rather I now move through my days (well, most of them) with a sense of flourishing, improving, and progressing. We can choose to survive in the midst of struggle and pain, and when we do, we reap the beautiful benefits of being resilient and enduring. We thrive!

When I think about this very tumultuous time, for my family and for me, I sometimes get fearful of it returning. I now know how to recognize it. I know what happens in my body when I begin to get caught up in the strive mentality. I begin to feel empty and depleted. Literally, my physical, emotional, mental, and spiritual energy is zapped. The "it" I am referring to is the hard, long, scary, dark time of anxiety and depression. It sort of blindsided me; I didn't see it coming. It just hit. I couldn't sleep; I couldn't concentrate; I felt "less than" at work and at home. I would not wish a trial like this on my worst enemy, but I am also so grateful God took me through this storm because I came out the other side for the better. I grew, my husband grew, and our kids grew. I did not hide any of my struggles from any of them. It was an open-book journey from the very beginning. God used this bad for His good. My kids learned that people will struggle in life; they, in fact, will struggle. And it's okay to ask for help, to accept help. We all learned that mental illness is real, and there should not be any shame attached to it. It is just as much an illness as asthma, diabetes, allergies, etc. I was able to learn an imperative lesson because I used to be one to think, "What do you mean you're anxious/depressed? What do you have to be anxious/depressed about?" Well, now I know. It just is. It just happens. And it is a nightmare to live through. But I learned to be less judgmental of others and myself. My husband learned the importance of slowing down, and he learned that he is not Superman. He can't fix everything. He couldn't "fix" me. He needed to sit with me, cry with me, and encourage me to have the courage to get the help I needed. We both learned that by our constant, incessant need to always be doing, our kids were inherently learning that trait. So we put every effort into helping them see otherwise. Because we showed them and specifically told them, our kids learned that we love them for them. For the gift, they are to us. For who they are and for what they feel. We love them for them, not what they do or don't do, not what they accomplish or don't, not what they win or don't, not any type of performance—just them! Wholeheartedly them!

It is a societal pressure that has been handed down from generation to generation, to generation. It was handed down to our parents, it was handed down to us, and here we are, a generation handing it down yet again. This is no fault and no blame game to any one generation; it is just the way we are wired as humans and as a country. The questions when first meeting someone sounds something like this: "Who are you?" "What do you do?" "Where do you work?" "What school do your kids go to?" What about my interests, my hobbies, and my passions? But then, as parents, as teachers, and as a society, we turn around and ask the same questions to the children in our lives. From the time these precious babies set foot in Kindergarten, we start bombarding them with the same types of questions: "Where do you go to school?" "What sports do you play?" "Where do you want to go to college?" and the infamous "What do you want to be when you grow up?" Ugh... societal pressure to do, do, DO, and perform rather than just BE. The "season" of anxiety and depression (I call it a season, but it is an everyday part of my life that I have to actively work on, and that's ok) that I stumbled through was a walk of humility. I was humbled by the realization that I couldn't be it all. I can't do it all. And guess what? I was never meant to. My work does not define my worth; my career is not my life calling. It is my career calling. It is one piece of me; not the entirety of me. My value is not my vocation; my vocation can shift from season to season. At this very moment, my vocations are wife, mom, daughter, sister, friend, and teacher. God uses these blessed vocations as a vehicle for me to BE me and follow my faith's call to love.

Here are a few of the warning signs that pop up on my striving radar:

- I do more, but I never feel like it's enough.
- I listen to my mind (task manager, negative talk, etc.) like it's my boss.
- I feel exhausted but can't shut my brain off to sleep.
- I work non-stop and have feelings of guilt when I take time off.

I now better know how to just BE. I am not going to lie; it is not always easy. I'm not perfect. It takes work, hard work. All good things in life require work- not the DOing work, but the BEing work. Remember, it's all about trying. Show up for your life, live your life. You only get this one, and the people who know you and love you need you. The world needs you. You were created for a purpose. God made you, and He makes no mistakes.

So now, I can sit with my "babies", ages 20, 18, 16, and 14, and my husband and have real conversations—conversations where we look into each other's eyes and really listen. Conversations that linger over dinner longer than I used to be able to sit and look at the war zone that was my kitchen. For you see, my friend, I have learned that BEing more present, BEing more patient, BEing more accepting, BEing more faith-filled, BEing more relaxed is far better than running myself ragged with all the DOing. I am living more freely than I ever have in my adult life, and my happiness shows it. I want to BE. I want to be the light, the smile, the hello, the eye contact, the "how are you?" that makes someone else's day a bit brighter.

I can simply *BE*. I don't have to DO.

And here is what it looks like when I am in thriving mode:

- My goals reflect my values, my interests, and my passions.
- I prioritize important people, projects, and hobbies in my life.
- I pause long enough to look around and take in my surroundings. I literally stop and do a 5-senses check. What do I see, hear, taste, smell, and feel in this exact moment?
- I carve out time at the end of my day to unwind—read, do yoga, pray, and journal.

What happened after I realized I could cease striving and avoid the mere survival of my days is I began to surrender and thrive. I experienced an opening up to others and to myself, and I began to break open. My breaking open led me to share my struggles with others. I no longer hide behind my perfecting, my pleasing, and my performing. I have broken open, and I am ready to share my whole self, my true self. I learned that it would be better for me to let God use my pain than to let my pain use me. I have learned to allow my growing seasons to move more freely. Like a river, I no longer resist or fear the flow. I have accepted that life is not linear. It is not straight up and down or left to right. Life is circular. I will flail as I learn, I will learn and succeed, and then something or someone new will come along, and I will learn and flail all over again. My goal is to pay attention to the pattern of my flow and learn from it. I have learned that God works on His time, not mine. His purposes are greater than what I have in mind or even what I first see when I consider what he is doing in my life. I have gained such growth in the area of surrender, ceasing to strive and resting in God. He knew busyness was a way of life for me, but he never leaves us how he finds us. He intervened. He came in the midst of my busy, self-

> He came in the midst of my busy, self-reliant, self-sufficient, self-righteous life, and little by little, He taught me that I am not enough. Not without Him.

reliant, self-sufficient, self-righteous life, and little by little, He taught me that I am not enough. Not without him. He drew me into a greater dependence on His wisdom and His plan for me, and He has helped me learn to let go. I had to come to the end of myself before I was willing to change, but I am grateful He met me at the end of my rope. He taught me that He loves me for me—not what I've done or what I will do. Just me, right here, right now. He taught me that I am worthy of his love, grace, mercy, compassion, and forgiveness. He bore it all on the cross for me. And he bore it for you too.

Scripture

Matthew 6:26-28, 34 *"Look at the birds of the air; they do not sow or reap or store away in barns, and yet your heavenly Father feeds them. Are you not much more valuable than they? Can any one of you by worrying add a single hour to your life? And why do you worry about clothes? See how the flowers of the field grow. They do not labor or spin."*

"Therefore, do not worry about tomorrow, for tomorrow will worry about itself. Each day has enough trouble of its own."

Reflection

What does it look like in your mind to thrive? Do you feel you are thriving during the majority of your day, or are you living in survival mode? Take time to write out your schedule for a typical day. Where are you checking items off your list for mere survival? Are there slots in your day where you are thriving?

_____

_____

_____

_____

Prayer

Our Father, who art in heaven, hallowed be thy name; thy kingdom come; thy will be done on earth as it is in heaven. Give us this day our daily bread, and forgive us our trespasses as we forgive those who trespass against us. And lead us not into temptation, but deliver us from evil.

Chapter 5:
Less Breaking Down, More Breaking Open

When we break open, we are letting the light shine in, and we are inviting others to break open too.

Sometimes, we humans, in all our good, concerted efforts, best of intentions, and determination to be the best version God has created us to be, lose sight that He is God and we are not. Sometimes we need to be reminded to be still, to lie down. In Psalm 23, we learn that our Good Shepherd makes us "lie down in green pastures" (Psalm 23:2). In this competitive, do more, do better, never enough society, we often feel that more is better. And when that happens, He is right there to let us know that less is quite enough. Oftentimes, He reminds us that in order to experience the good in this life, we must also endure hardships. I've heard it said that 'for beauty to come from ashes, something's got to burn.'

> I've heard it said that 'for beauty to come from ashes, something's got to burn.'

I don't in any way believe that God is one to shake his finger at us. But I do believe that He uses struggles, uncertainties, challenges, and obstacles to teach, restore, renew, and refine us. He made it very clear that in this life, we will have trouble. I believe that when we go through a season of hardship, it is often God's way of getting our attention—a spiritual wake-up call, so to speak. It's His rap on our knuckles to remind us to live life fully with Him at the helm.

Five years ago, when I found myself in the deep, dark depths of what seemed like an insurmountable struggle, God was wrapping my knuckles. He was giving me a much-needed wake-up call. For all intents and purposes, one might listen to my description of what I struggled through, wrestled with, and fought and immediately coin it a "mid-life crisis" or "mental breakdown." I, too, called it those things at the time. But after walking through the fire, not without burns, and surviving the storm, I fully know that what I experienced was not a breakdown. It was me breaking open. After plodding through that tumultuous journey, I am more myself, more comfortable in my own skin, and more at peace than I have been at any other point in my life.

It was late May of 2017; school was out for the summer, and my family had an exciting trip to the Southwest planned for early June. We would be flying from Cincinnati to Denver, where we would begin the journey of driving over 3,000 miles to take in the glorious sights of seven different national parks. As most moms do, I was experiencing feelings of anxiety in the days leading up to the trip. I kept trying to stuff the feelings down and remind myself that it's always high stress right before a big trip. "Jodi, calm down," I would tell myself. But this time felt different. It was a restlessness that was affecting my daily functioning, focus, and sleep. Looking back, I remember telling Matt that something was off. I explained it as being "on edge."

Remind you, school was out for the summer, and I am a teacher. I typically take a huge sigh of relief at this time of year. But I wasn't, not in the least. I couldn't even take a full breath. I gave my parents a heads-up that I was feeling off; I assured them I was okay and that I was not calling to worry them but that I simply wanted their prayers for my peace. I also shared my feelings with my doctor, as I thought, being in my early forties, that there may be some hormonal explanation. She assured me that I was too young to be experiencing pre-menopausal symptoms. With more wisdom, research, and other doctors' opinions, I now know more and don't agree with her "too young" response. She told me to call her when I returned from the trip, and she could prescribe an anti-anxiety medication to see if that helped. So, off I went on what was sure to be one of the happiest adventures of a lifetime with Matt and the kids.

It was not an adventure in any fun sense of the word for me; rather, it was an adventure of me grasping to wrangle in my anxiety, my sleeplessness, and compulsiveness. It was me always having my eye out for the closest hospital, urgent care, or ranger station, all while trying to paste a smile on my face and appear to Matt and the kids that I was having the time of my life. I should rewind here a bit and explain that I have a heart condition that has required a few medical procedures and medication. I was obsessing over a story I had created in my own mind. One where we would be out hiking, and I would collapse, or we would be midflight, and I would suffer a heart attack. Both of these stories had endings of me not getting the help I needed in time to survive. Every scenario I created in my mind included me leaving Matt and the kids way too soon. Missing out on things like watching their sporting events, enjoying each other around the firepit on Saturday nights, sending them off for the first time as they drove the car out of the driveway, dating, high school dances, graduations, weddings, life. I kept telling myself, "Jodi, it's fine. I am fine. Everything is fine." But it wasn't. This period of ongoing insomnia led to my long, dark, and scary period of crippling anxiety and depression.

When we returned from our trip, I waited a few weeks before calling my doctor about the anti-anxiety medication. I remember calling her the 4th of July weekend while we were visiting our family in Connecticut. She listened to my symptoms and called in an order for the medication. Well, I took that for two nights and refused to ever take it again. It made me feel like I was completely coming undone. I was tremoring and shaking; I was pacing like a caged animal; I was having the darkest, scariest, most bizarre thoughts a person could have. I figured if I was having such a horrific response to the medication, then surely I must not need it. So, I stopped taking it. Period. The End.

But the sleepless nights, incessant worry, and depression did not stop. No period. No End.

And my grasping, my desperation, my attempt to fix it all did not end either.

Fast forward to October of 2017 when I was not listening to my sleepless body. I was hiding how bad my struggle had become from everyone except Matt. I had shared bits and pieces here and there with my parents, Matt's parents, and a few of my close friends. But no one, except Matt, knew that I was up every night from 1 AM until the alarm went off at 5 AM; no one but Matt knew I was crying every morning, every night, and throughout most of my time at school. I literally hid in my classroom or the restroom and cried EVERY DAY. Then, one day, I remember it like it was yesterday, Friday, October 6th of 2017. I found myself at my desk before my students arrived for the day, unable to remember the password for my computer, unable to use the key to unlock my filing cabinet, unable to start planning for the next week, and unable to think at all. The only thing my body allowed me to do was to call Dana, my dear, loving friend of fifteen years who taught in the school with me. She answered, but I couldn't speak. My sobbing on the other end was all she needed to hear. She immediately came to my room, got me and my things, and drove me home. I remember trying to control that scenario too. I had a meeting that morning I needed to attend; it was Homecoming weekend for Anna; my in-laws were in town; I had ETR and IEP documents to get ready for a meeting that following Monday. But she didn't have time for talk; she was in full-blown, best friend, beast mode, and she was going to get me out of there. She got me home, hugged me goodbye, and my in-laws cared for me from there. The weekend passed, and I, of course, returned to work on Monday. My amazing leader, the principal of the school, and my friend came to me and encouraged me to take time to rest, rejuvenate, and care for myself.

She urged me to take a two-week leave of absence so I could see my doctor and begin sorting out and working through all the hurdles I was facing.

What seems like a sudden, overnight change was a journey long in the making. I went from over-performing and producing to numbing out doing nothing at all. I was an overachieving, high-functioning person riddled with anxiety, and I was just too busy to recognize it. Until God used my lack of sleep, my exhaustion, and my crippling anxiety to shut it all down. I broke down- this was not a choice. It was desperation and full-throttle survival mode. I had to stop everything. I had to break down, physically and mentally, before God could get to my mind and heart and beautifully break me open. I had *sources*: my family, my friends, my neighbors, and coworkers, and God. But, by breaking me open, God helped me realize I needed *resources*. I needed to rely on others; I needed to be willing to ask for help and receive it. I needed counseling and medication. Looking back, I now realize I've always had anxiety. It just showed up as pleasing, performing, controlling, and managing.

> **I had to break down, physically and mentally, before God could get to my mind and heart and beautifully break me open.**

I spent from the second week of October 2017 to January 2018 doing just that. I stepped away from work and got the help, rest, and care I needed. I finally started getting some sleep, which was in and of itself a Godsend. But more importantly, I had the time to dig deep enough to realize that the one person I had not yet really talked to about all of this, the one person I had not asked for any specific guidance or advice, was THE ONE that could save me from it all. God. Sure, I had pleaded to Him, "God, please!" "Why, God?" "What is this for, God?" But I had not surrendered to Him. Rather, I was putting all of my faith and trust in my own actions—my own do-all, be-all, fix-all mentality. When, in fact, I needed to step aside and do less, so God could take the reigns and do more.

I struggled with this because "less" means of lower rank or importance, and I didn't like to think of myself as "less than." I did not struggle with accepting that I am/was less than God or that He is greater than me. And, although it was a brown, withered seed, I did have every faith that He would pull me out of the muck and the mire. But, boy, oh boy, did I struggle with the time and patience that it took. Time and patience to start getting decent sleep at night; time and patience to find a counselor that I felt comfortable with and that shared my love for Jesus; time and patience to find the just right medication and the just right dose; and time and patience to accept myself, accept my struggle, accept my need for help; accept my humanness; and time and patience to rid myself of the shame and be willing to share my struggle with others. And last, but certainly, not least, time and patience to study His word; I mean really study it. Read it, write it, ask Him questions, and seek His guidance. I scour it for verses that would speak life into my soul at the time. In my season of feverishly searching, a verse that has always been familiar to me suddenly "came to me" (that's the Holy Spirit). Romans 5:3-4 says, "...but we also glory in our sufferings because we know that suffering produces perseverance; perseverance, character; and character, hope." I quickly realized that the words were there, all of them. Right there in print. Words that can affirm, uplift, nourish, and save. And guess what? I didn't have to scour for them; He very clearly spoke to me through the wisdom of others. Whether it be Matt, my dad, my friends, my counselor, a co-worker that was, and still is, a pillar of strength and spiritual mentorship to me, or in my daily devotionals, and Bible readings, His hands were all over my struggling, growing, and flourishing. Right where I was struggling the most and feeling torn to pieces, right in the middle of the hard, ugly mess, was where I most found Jesus and His unending peace.

> Right where I was struggling the most and feeling torn to pieces, right in the middle of the hard, ugly mess, was where I most found Jesus and His unending peace.

It was like he was calling out to me, "Come to me, Jodi. Rest in my arms. Be still and know that I am your God, and I will never leave you or forsake you." The words were there when I needed them, right when I needed them the most, and I believe, dear friend, they always have been. But, I needed to slow down, to break open my heart for God and His words.

As I struggled with becoming "less," in the sense that I was taking time off work, I was relying on others (i.e., doctors, counselors) to help me, I was struggling in front of my kids, and I was leaning on Matt harder than I ever had in our sixteen years of marriage. I also grew more than at any other time in my life. Progress is made through purpose and intention, and we often need a push to take those steps. The time off that my principal "pushed" me to take was just what I needed. I had the time I needed to pursue God, pursue professional help, and pursue myself. In order to fully understand His "highness" and the light that He shines, I had to go low; I had to see the darkness. And all the while, throughout this breakdown and what felt like a ripping apart of my soul, I was actually breaking open. My mind and my heart were opening up to what it means to endure and have resiliency. The strength I was gaining was producing my character and, through my character, hope. My hope in God and all I knew He could do in and through me in this trial.

A few of the Scriptures that anchored my heart during this difficult time and remain some of my most revisited verses are:

- Devote yourselves to prayer, being watchful and thankful. (Colossians 4:2)
- Be joyful in hope, patient in affliction, and faithful in prayer. (Romans 12:12)
- For I know the plans I have for you, declares the Lord, plans to prosper you and not harm you, plans to give you hope and a future. (Jeremiah 29:11)

- He lifted me out of the slimy pit, out of the mud and mire; he set my feet on a rock and gave me a firm place to stand. (Psalm 40:2)

- For I am the Lord your God who takes hold of your right hand and says to you, Do not fear; I will help you. (Isaiah 41:13)

Part of this pursuit of wholeness and coming out of the darkness and into the light included me being transparent about what I was going through. Being vulnerable used to scare the daylights out of me, but this journey—this breaking open—gave me the wisdom to see that breaking open is not the same as breaking down. Breaking open allowed me to make room for something new. The something new was a more vulnerable, less than perfect me, an honest me, a me that threw aside the shame over what I was going through and opened myself up to others. I began to learn that how and what I feel is more important than what others think of me. Sharing my story, letting others in, showing that I am not perfect, I don't have everything together all the time, and I can't perform or perfect any longer, and I do need help, breaks me open to others, and it lets them in. Letting them in allows me to point others to Jesus. It allows them to see His strength in my weakness. Learning to let go of who I thought I was supposed to be and accepting and loving who I truly am has allowed me to build connections and community with others that I would have normally never gotten to know. It bridges gaps and tears down the comparative walls I and others have worked so hard to build. I have learned that being exposed, and having the courage to bare our souls, is, in fact, the only way to experience real growth.

> I have learned that being exposed, and having the courage to bare our souls, is, in fact, the only way to experience real growth.

The biggest area of growth that came from my breaking open was my recognition and understanding of my own feelings. Before my breaking open, and probably what led to it, I was the master of stuffing my feelings away. I could compartmentalize my feelings just as efficiently as I organized my drawers and checked items off my to-do lists. I would feel something or begin to feel it—love, anger, envy, frustration, vulnerability, loneliness—then I would shove it in a drawer (a well-organized one at that) and charge on. Head down, nose to the grindstone, keep moving, keep working, keep hustling and getting it done, whatever it was. I wore this like a badge of honor. "Look at me; look how strong I am. I don't need help. I don't have bad days. Look how much I can endure and still stand." But then all those feelings, bubbling underneath the surface, exploded! They all came gushing through and out, and I didn't know what to do with them.

What I thought was warrior woman living, my counselor taught me, was emotionally unhealthy. I thought if I felt sad, mad, hurt, angry, frustrated, overwhelmed, or any of the "negative" emotions, then I was bad. Only a lonely person feels lonely. Only a sad person feels sad. Only an angry person feels angry. But now I know, a person surrounded by loving family and friends can feel lonely, a very happy and content person can feel sad, and a joy-filled, easy-going person can feel angry. It's called being human. So I have grown, my feelings have grown, and they have permission to exist. My feelings are real; I am real. I no longer pretend anymore, and guess what? I don't feel emotionally exhausted all the time because my emotions are alive, they have a breath, and they have a say. During my breaking open, when I was zoomed in on the struggle, all I could see and feel was shame. I viewed myself as flawed; I was embarrassed, and I felt alone in my struggle. But as I grew and allowed my feelings to grow and show, all I could see was that I was surrounded by people enduring the same types of struggle. And we all had common factors of resiliency. I had to stay present and mindful of my feelings and remind myself of my resiliency and the support that surrounded me. Once I realized I wasn't all alone, I moved forward one day at a time, knowing that I couldn't go back and make all the details pretty, but I could take the next step, face each day, and create something beautiful by piecing myself back together again. I had to lean into the discomfort and hard emotions. Do I feel more vulnerable and less perfect? Yes. Do I feel more alive, more real, more tender, and true? 100% yes!

In the midst of my breaking open, when I thought it was still very much a breaking down, I remember finding strength and the will to persevere through the idea of "God, if you help me, if you'll rescue me from this storm and wake me from this nightmare, then I will do all I can to share you with others. I will live for you, and I will live to help others. Even if my story helps save only one other person, then it will be worth all the pain and suffering." My questions and pleas turned from "Why me? How much longer? When will it be over?" to "How are you going to use this for good, God? Even if it's for the good of helping someone else, then it is a cross I am willing to bear."

Even if... That "even if" I prayed and pleaded every day to God became a reality—and I have been able to share my story with friends, family, and even strangers. And my story, my willingness to share it, and my feelings, reactions, and responses to it have opened the doors to God's light being able to shine in the dark spaces of others. A few years after I came through my storm, a woman I know through teaching reached out to me. She messaged me on Facebook and shared that she was going through a very dark, scary time, and she wondered if I could give her a call. I was thrilled—not that she was hurting, of course—that God was using my struggle to help someone else. I replied to her right away and said I would love to talk with her—or, more importantly, just be a listening ear. What I thought would be a brief phone conversation turned into more than an hour of her sharing her hurt, fears, and pain. I listened, asked clarifying questions, let her know I saw her and understood her pain, and then prayed with her. She shared that she admired my faith and how it was clear in my social media posts that my relationship with God was what got me through. She asked how I did that, "How did you hold onto God and trust Him when you were in your lowest, darkest moments?" I don't know where my response came from, but I recall saying without hesitation, "I didn't know how much I needed God until I realized He was all I ever truly had." And all I heard on the other end of what became a quiet interaction was her audible cry. I, too, was quiet because my answer took me by surprise. It's like the Holy Spirit himself answered for me.

Fast forward to the fall of 2022, and I got a phone call from her again. I admit my heart sank a bit as I was fearful of what she may need or be going through. Well, it was a lot. She was living every parent's worst nightmare. She called to let me know her child, who was receiving mental health care in an inpatient facility, had taken her own life. I was stunned, speechless. I had no words other than "I'm so sorry" to say to her. My words could not fix or make better the utterly unimaginable situation she faced. In spite of all she was going through—all the hurt, suffering, and pain—she called to let me know that my prayers over her and my support and willingness to be open and honest about my struggle with anxiety and depression were continuing to help her in the midst of the worst storm of her life. She shared that she was reminded of me telling her that "we don't know how much we need God until we see He is all we really have."

Just as in the Book of Isaiah, when God promised His people that He would bring them back into the Promised Land, He will make a way through all of our sufferings. Our suffering is never in vain. When we are trapped in suffering, mourning, pain, waiting, and loneliness, just as I felt I was, it can feel as if it is lasting far too long. This darkness in the tunnel that seems to have no end can cause tension, anxiety, and fear. Problems are bound to surface somewhere along our life's journey. But we must accept, face, and deal with the challenges that He purposefully puts on our paths. Because what I have learned is that this journey is not about me. It is about Him–His goodness, His glory, His purpose, and His power. We must trust that all things, even suffering, will be used for His good. We are promised an abundant life, not a life free of troubles. The suffering we endure today will be the catalyst that increases our

> The suffering we endure today will be the catalyst that increases our faith tomorrow.

faith tomorrow. Keep walking, friend. God will see you through this—whatever your "this" is. Our job is to keep our eyes on Jesus and keep pointing others to Him, thanking Him for leading us and carrying us through our deserts when we can't bare to take another step.

When we break open, we open our hearts to others, we share our story and our pain, our vulnerability, so they don't feel so alone. By sharing our story, we just might save someone. The problem is, once we have broken open, we must accept our vulnerability and learn that life is not about being happy. Happiness is dependent on our happenings, and our happenings of everyday life will fail us and leave us falling short every time. Real living and true life are about abundant joy that comes from deep within. It is our owning and defining of the current state we find ourselves. We don't let our circumstances define us. (More on this later.)

Friends, sharing our stories, sharing our faith, sharing our hope and trust in Jesus matters. It makes a difference. As we journey through life, facing obstacles, struggles, setbacks, and pain, may we be reminded that God uses it all for good. He wastes nothing. My prayer is that my words, my vulnerable sharing, will point others straight to Him. So let us share our hurts, our pains, knowing that we are doing so for the good of others and for His glory.

Brokenness does not have to lead to shame. Brokenness most often leads to beauty. Those "things" that began to bother me during my brokenness always had. I was just too busy hiding from my true feelings. I was too busy being busy and making everything look just so. When I broke, I saw myself. The light was pouring in from all the cracks, and I could see, truly see, for likely the first time in my life, who I was and who I am. The real me. Not the do it all, all the time, for all the people me. Just me, Jodi. My anxiety and depression left me with bumps and bruises; it was a journey I never asked for but one I will be forever grateful for having been given. Yes, I have times

> **Brokenness does not have to lead to shame. Brokenness most often leads to beauty.**

84

when I fear I will go back to that awful dark place, but my counselor assures me that I won't. "You've learned too much; you've grown too much to ever go all the way back," she tells me. And my Savior reminds me that He is with me. He watches over me and holds me in His loving hands, so if I do "go back," I know He goes before me, He goes with me, and He won't leave me in the fiery furnace alone. He is with us in our vulnerability. He is not surprised by a single step of our journey. He is not afraid. I can say things out loud to Him, and it is so freeing. I can even shout in anger at Him. By being open with Jesus and with others, I am drawing people closer to me. I am more approachable and more real. And when others draw closer to me, my prayer is I am drawing them closer to God.

While I wouldn't wish my struggle on anyone, and I wade through fear of going back there myself, I would go back and relive it over and over if it meant I would grow closer to God, I could point others to Jesus, and others that are suffering would emerge from the darkness and into the light with me. The enemy wants us to live in the past. He wants us to have regrets and carry shame for the difficulties we have endured. But God. God wants us to live in the present, surrounded and comforted by His perfect peace. I can think of nothing more lovely than to be beautifully broken alongside others. What if we all let go of the idea of perfection? What if we all realized we are not perfect, but we are real? What would happen if we all allowed ourselves to be flawed and make mistakes? Wouldn't life be so much easier, so much lighter, if we accepted that we're not always going to have it all together, sometimes our hearts are going to break, and we're going to face pain, grief, and suffering? And what if we stopped apologizing for our pain, our tears, our brokenness? Because when we share our brokenness, we become more alive, more real, and more relatable. We understand ourselves better, and others see more of us—more of our

> **Because when we share our brokenness, we become more alive, more real, and more relatable.**

truth, more of our hurts, more of our strength and resiliency. To be broken means we let life in, all the good and the bad, we let our feelings in, and we let others in. I have learned through my brokenness. My heart is heavy. I feel pain, grief, and disappointment now more than ever, but I also love more deeply, I live more freely, and I appreciate the shiny, glowing joy of the beauty that is life. Through my struggle and brokenness, I have developed a sense of self and of others. I am more compassionate and empathetic. I understand the pain others are facing because I finally faced my own. When I was controlling my life, stuffing away, hiding, and ignoring my emotions, not allowing myself to feel, I was breaking down. I was in a constant state of being tired, frustrated, and anxious, and at times I completely numbed out or went into freeze mode. And when I started closing my heart off to pain, it also closed my heart's capacity to feel true love, happiness, and joy. I don't look forward to the struggles and difficult times that come in life and break our hearts wide open. But I also don't live in fear or dread of them either. I know they are going to come- they are inevitable. So I choose now to embrace them with a fully opened heart because if I choose to close off my heart to fully feel the pain and the hurt, then I am also choosing to close off my heart to fully feel the love and joy that is this life.

For most of us, there will come a time in our lives when we fall so hard that getting back up will seem impossible. And as much as I fear slipping back to that dark place, facing other difficult times, or watching as a loved one struggles, I know I can face it with greater strength and wisdom than before. I am equipped to handle future adversities. Because of breaking open before, I am now permanently open. I am open with more insight and humility, open with greater strength and resiliency, and open with deeper faith and trust.

When you face adversity, it's worth asking yourself:

Will I break down, or will I break open?

Will I be open to gaining wisdom in the midst of this storm?

Will I face this trial with eyes wide open and thrive? Or will I numb out, freeze, and merely survive?

Along with gray hairs, deeper laugh lines, and an inability to stay awake past 10 PM, my forties have brought me wisdom. I am softer, slower, quieter, and calmer. I can see more clearly now what matters most. And I show up as the real me. The me that God created and intended for me to be. The me that gives Him all the glory and honor He is due. Our lives come to a stop whether we choose them to or our circumstances cause them to. I believe with my whole being that God brought me to a full stop six years ago to wake me up, to shake me into alertness and awareness of what He had in store for me. He wants us to be attentive and receptive to what He is doing in and through our lives, not how much we can do. And, He wants us to be aware that His work through us is working in the lives of others as well. I am certain my suffering and my pain have helped countless others along the way. And I will continue to share my sufferings, all of my days, if it means sharing the love of Jesus.

And I will continue to share my sufferings, all of my days, if it means sharing the love of Jesus.

Scripture

Romans 5:3-4 *"Not only so, but we also glory in our sufferings, because we know that suffering produces perseverance; perseverance, character; and character, hope."*

2 Corinthians 4:8-9 *"We are hard pressed on every side, but not crushed; perplexed, but not in despair; persecuted, but not abandoned; struck down, but not destroyed."*

Romans 12:12
"Be joyful in hope, patient in affliction, faithful in prayer."

Reflection

Do you find yourself faking and/or stuffing your feelings? Why do you hesitate to open up to others with your true feelings? Do you feel your feelings define you? Why? Do you think you would feel less stressed/less "heavy" if you were open and honest about your feelings, shared them with others, and talked about them? Why? How can you begin to process and feel your feelings more openly and honestly? Who are two people in your life that you will be more open with?

_____

_____

_____

_____

Prayer

Heavenly Father, I come before you to lay my anxiety and depression at your feet. When I feel as if I am being washed away by the waves of my worries, fears, and sadness, help me remember that you are my refuge and savior. Fill me with your peace as I learn to trust in you and you alone. You are my rock and my protector, and you have blessed me with loving, supportive family and friends. Help me open up, be more vulnerable, and let these wonderful people carry my burdens with me. Give me the wisdom to seek what you would do and the courage to do that. Lift from me the need to achieve all and surrender to what you want to be in me.

Chapter 6: Less Happy, More Joy

Joyful living comes from a place and practice of gratitude, and the power of joy comes from someone higher and greater than you or me–it comes from God.

One of the greatest gifts that came from my breaking open is that I learned to value joy and contentment over happiness. I learned the difference between happiness and joy. Happiness is reliant upon our happenings, and joy is from God. Joy can be with us all the time, regardless of our circumstances. I have learned that I need to stop waiting for everything to be perfect in order for me to be "happy." I have learned that I need to treasure the ordinary moments of everyday life rather than white-knuckling my days into perfect, extraordinary events. I have learned that I need to be able to trust God and see His goodness in all things—ordinary things—regardless of whether or not I am happy. When we fight and struggle against the natural flow of happenings in our lives and what our lives are offering us, the joy will inevitably get snuffed out of us. Joy is God's light, buried in every dark crevice, shining forth, illuminating us from

> Joy is God's light, buried in every dark crevice, shining forth, illuminating us from the inside out regardless of our circumstances.

the inside out regardless of our circumstances.

What about you, reader? Do you find yourself happy when things are going great and everything is smooth sailing? Do you feel "meh" when things aren't happening quite as you planned? We're all going to have days when we feel we're on top of the world, our mountain top, flex our muscles kind of days. And, I'm here to tell you that we're also all going to have days, weeks, or seasons when it seems we can't get out of the valley—when all seems lost and dark and lonely and scary. Will we feel happy during these dark seasons? Probably not. Can we experience the peace and comfort of joy? Yes. Absolutely! In recent years, I have been learning and contemplating more deeply about my pursuit of happiness versus my finding peace in the joy of life itself.

Real happiness is about allowing and navigating the difficult times of life. Just as the tide ebbs and flows, it's natural for us to experience waves, roller coaster rides, and mountaintop highs and valley lows. That's just life. Don't fight it. Ride the waves, go with the flow. The fighting just causes a constant state of anxiety and fear and anger, and disappointment. Trying to avert or ignore the harder times just makes the joy of life even less attainable. Real happiness is about allowing and navigating the difficult times of life. We cannot control everything that happens in our lives. There are circumstances beyond our control: a diagnosis, the death of a loved one, a spouse walking out the door, or the loss of a job, but we can control our response and our reaction to those difficult times. I long to be more reflective, more responsive, and less reactive. I want to hold tight to the steadfast love of Jesus, where I know I will find more than happiness. I will find joy. We can't stop the bad from happening, and we certainly can't tell it how or when to strike. But we can control our response in our reaction to bad times. I don't know about you, but I have spent much of my life dodging bullets, playing it safe, and avoiding disaster. I wore myself out reacting histrionically to every gone wrong situation. I have grown and learned; I have accepted the fact that bad things will happen to me and my loved ones. The difference now is that I want to be more open, more accepting of these things, the hard, bad things of life. I want to save myself hours and days of worrying, controlling, and managing and simply take the days as they come. Doesn't that sound much less exhausting? I want it for you too. Let's do our best not to be overwhelmed or discouraged by the days' or weeks' challenges. May we find the faith and grace to overcome everything that comes our way. May we trust that God will give us enough for each day—manna. Let's stop waiting for everything to be perfect to be happy. If we live this way, we will be waiting a very long time. There's no such thing as a perfect life. There's only the willingness to embrace the precious, imperfect life with which we have been blessed.

> **May we trust that God will give us enough for each day-manna.**

Coming out of my breaking open, and a year later, experiencing the sudden loss of my dad, I knew that I had grown spiritually and that I was rooted more in joy from God's abundant blessings, and that happiness was something that I wouldn't feel all the time, not even most of the time. And I was okay with that. I was okay with settling into uncomfortable feelings and hard times. I had learned to realize that life is a precious gift, and I learned to accept it as just that. A gift, regardless of my circumstances. I am proud of my learning, my growth, and my transformative view of everyday living. I am settling into the idea that God is the author of my story. And that no matter what the events of my story are, Jesus can and will use it all for good. Nothing in my life is too messed up or too far gone for Him. He can take all things and make them new, he can and will use them for good. He has and will continue to use my story, and yours, as a story of restoration, a story of redemption, a story of love. That's what life is, isn't it? One big, messy, hard, fun, wild ride of all of life's ups and downs. But we must remember that God is good all the time, and all the time God is good.

I grew to know this, even more, when the entire world came to a hard stop in March 2020. Matt and I were enjoying a vacation just the two of us in the Pacific Northwest. We had visited Portland, Vancouver, and were in our last stop, Seattle, when we got the news that the world was closing down. Schools were closing, borders were closing and we were desperate to get home to our kids. What started as a few weeks of being out of school turned into a very scary, isolating, trying six months of everybody at home all day, every day. COVID-19 took over and took away our freedoms as we knew them to be. Life as we knew it no longer existed. Schools, workplaces, churches, stores, restaurants, even outdoor parks—everything—were closed. Other things were canceled—proms, graduations, sporting events, weddings, vacations, and even funerals. It was so eerie, so wild, so unknown. It was a time that most people, including myself, would not have classified as happy. I'll admit I didn't feel overly optimistic about the situation our world was in, and I certainly would not describe what was happening all around us—closures, cancellations, job losses, and numerous deaths—as happy. But I found joy; I had joy. I had a sense of peace that God was doing what God does best, and He was working all things together for the good of those who love Him. He was taking messes and making messages. He was using what the enemy intended for evil for His good.

Joy is the very breath that supports us in doing hard things. It's okay to laugh when sadness is all around us. We can hold joy and sorrow, bliss and grief, laughter and tears, pleasure and despair. When faced with tough times, we have to look for joy, find joy and create joy. We have to make it happen by realizing the beauty in what God has already given us. We have to fall in love with what we have and let go of what we don't. When I was deep in my pit of despair, shrouded in anxiety and depression, I had to look for and see the joy of Jesus in the eyes and smiles of Matt and the kids. When my dad was taken from us too soon, I had to dig deep into my well of joy. I had to share, listen as others shared, and celebrate and remember what

> **We have to fall in love with what we have and let go of what we don't.**

an amazing man he was and how I was so fortunate and so blessed to have called him mine. My Dad, "Pap" to my kids, my support. And then COVID-19, another life circumstance that tested me. "Are you going to look for, find, and create joy, Jodi?" And I did. Matt, the kids, and I took full advantage of this forced time together. We had cooking contests, shared stories and laughs around our fire pit, and we had more days and nights of consecutive backyard fun than we can even count. Were there times we were frustrated, scared, annoyed, irritated, and disappointed? Yes. Yes. And YES! We certainly had times of feeling guilty about our "happy days" when the world was suffering. But…God. But… Joy! We can't give joy or share it with others if we don't have it ourselves. We can be joyful and grateful while also recognizing the pain and suffering in our lives, the lives of others, and the world. So, turn on the music, break out your best dance moves, light the candles, make the cake, pour the wine, and throw the party.

Sorrow shows us what we love, what we don't want to lose. I was so sad and scared during the height of my anxiety/depression, but God was so good to show me who and what I love, especially Matt and the kids, and I was not about to let them be taken from me. I was going to look this scary, sad situation in the face, stare it down, and dare it to take me away from them, my purest joy.

When we struggle to take our thoughts captive, we need to be reminded over and over again of all that is good and right in this world and in our lives. Our feelings are not always an accurate measure of what is true.

Our feelings are not always an accurate measure of what is true.

The Bible doesn't tell us to focus only on what makes us happy or feel good. Sometimes, what is true is not happy and doesn't feel good. In fact, oftentimes, it's hard. But we can put hard things into perspective by focusing on what is right and true—and on Jesus, our one true Savior. He is our most precious and free gift of pure joy.

There is arguably no greater example of this kind of faith, hope, and joy in, and thankfulness for God than what Paul exudes in his letter to the Philippians. Paul wrote this letter to encourage church unity (Philippians 1:27-2:18), freedom from legalism (Philippians 3:2-21), salvation (Philippians 2:6-8), stewardship (Philippians 4:10-20), and imitation of Christ's humility (Philippians 2:5-11). His sentiments to the converts in Philippi are a reminder that our joy does not come from life's circumstances but from God alone. It's difficult for us to grasp just how faithful Paul was to God throughout his time in prison because most of us have never experienced this degree of persecution. Paul found strength in knowing that through his imprisonment, God was being magnified. Paul's faith is the optimism that got him through this ordeal. Whether he lived or died, whether he was appreciated or not, Paul wanted Christ to be honored. The whole book of Philippians helps us understand what it means to be Christlike. I have often heard it referred to as the "happy book" of the Bible. It is a short, only four chapters book in the Bible, but is full of joy and loving encouragement. Paul is not out in nature engaged in his favorite pastime, he is not surrounded by his beloved family and friends, and he is not enjoying his favorite foods or taking an unforgettable journey. No, he is in prison, but he is free of chains. Paul's joy comes only from Christ. In this book, Paul teaches us that joy often comes in the form of persecution. Paul was encouraging the people of Philippi, who were very proud of their earthly citizenship, to find joy in heavenly citizenship. If Paul can find joy in the Lord while in prison, can't we find it in our blessed lives? Paul said, "For to me, to live is Christ and to die is gain" (Philippians 1:21). Paul was acknowledging the fact that to die and be with Christ in eternity is far better than to live. But, he was always recognizing and pointing out that to live means we have fruitful work to do here on earth. Paul is reminding us that we will be mocked, scorned, rejected, and persecuted for Christ's name and our belief in Him. If you were in prison, like Paul, would you be able to show joy and preach on humility, unity, and contentment? I ask myself this often to keep my sense of joy in perspective.

It is natural to have highs and lows in life. We just need to learn to inhale the highs and hold on through the lows. That's just life. We can't wish away or ignore the lows. The more we fight them the harder they crash down on us. We need to learn to ride the waves or we will be in a constant, uphill battle. Swimming against the stream of life, being battered and washed over again and again with waves of anxiety, anger, frustration, depression, and disappointment. I pray that we, like Paul in the Book of Philippians, recognize and honor the life-changing power and saving grace of Jesus Christ. Paul endured suffering, sacrifice, and struggle, yet he still says in Philippians 4:12 that he knows how to have little and how to have a lot. May God's strength be our joy, and may our message be, "In Christ, I have all I need."

Below is an entry from my journal written in August 2020. This entry reflects how, while our happenings do not produce happiness, we can still find joy. When life seems so redundant, so boring, and so ordinary it is then we often experience the most extraordinary goodness of God's grace and love.

The last five months have been anything but ordinary. There have been very few things about life that have been commonplace, standard, or status quo since March 13th. In fact, I would label the last five months as containers of distinction, each holding its own unique qualities. I know where your mind is going… frustration, boredom, disappointment, sad, worn out! But that is not where I am going. After some reading and reflecting, I would dare to say the last five months have held some things that are quite extraordinary. They have been containers that have held nightly family dinners (all six of us at the same time—this never happens!), bike rides and hikes with Matt, the kids, and Max, baseball in the cul-de-sac, more practice driving time with Jack, extra soccer training in the backyard for Anna and Maggie, family game nights, slow mornings on the deck with hot, comforting coffee and evenings lingering around the fire, with my favorite wine in hand, talking, laughing and listening to music, cooking and baking lessons, laundry lessons, time. Time to breathe and connect. TIME—just the six of us.

I don't know about you, but the majority of the circumstances that the Pandemic has gifted me (yes, I said "gifted") have made me realize that my life, my people, and my own self are anything but ordinary. I have been re-awakened to the specialness of simply being. Being with myself. Being with God. Being with Matt. Being with Anna. Being with Jack. Being with Abby. Being with Maggie. And, yes, being with Max. Just being. All the forced time at home, and my rather empty family calendar, have afforded me and my people time together. Time we would have never had or taken. Time we will never get back. Time we will never forget. We learned that when we're with the people we love, those that matter most to us, the most ordinary things become extraordinary.

I have been reawakened to the specialness of simply being.

We learned that when we're with the people we love, those that matter most to us, the most ordinary things become extraordinary.

Our time in "Pandemic Prison" is quickly coming to an end. Matt and I are excitedly headed back to teach our classrooms full of kids; our own kids are headed back to school, and their sports seasons are gearing up, and it seems as if everyone is emerging out of their cocoons of life, ready to fly. It will be so easy to slip back into the rut of routines and schedules; the same 'ol same 'ol. So, I am setting an intention to keep finding joy in the ordinary. If I've learned anything in the last five months, it's that there's a lot of beauty in the ordinary things of life. And it's easy, and it's ordinary to love the good life, the happy life, the struggle-free life, the beautiful life. But it's more beautiful and rewarding to love the ordinary life. The ups and downs, the highs and the lows. I believe the ordinary

I believe that struggles and hardships prepare us, ordinary people, for extraordinary futures.

people, activities, moments, and thoughts in our lives are God's way of showing up for us and in us. I believe that struggles and hardships prepare us, ordinary people, for extraordinary futures.

So, if you feel inadequate, frustrated, weak, done, or discouraged by the last five months, be encouraged. If you feel overwhelmed because you've been trying so hard to do something great for your family, your friends, yourself, or God, give it a rest. Be proud of how you have handled the difficulties life has handed you- the silent, and not so silent, battles you have fought, the times when all you could do was sit and cry alone, celebrate your strength. Your ordinary, day-to-day living is quite extraordinary.

If we want to be used by God, all we have to do is walk the life He has laid before us and watch as He does extraordinary things through our seemingly ordinary lives. And, above all else, "Trust in the Lord with all your heart and lean not on your own understanding"

If we want to be used by God, all we have to do is walk the life He has laid before us and watch as He does extraordinary things through our seemingly ordinary lives.

(Proverbs 3:5). Remember that joyful living comes from a place and practice of gratitude, and the power of joy comes from someone higher and greater than you or me—it comes from God. Joy is all around us; we just need to train our eyes to look for and see it. And always, always remember the best life–not the happy life–but the most alive life, the most joyous life, the most extraordinary moments are found in ordinary, everyday life.

Scripture

Colossians 4:2 *"Devote yourselves to prayer, being watchful and thankful."*

John 10:10 *"The thief comes only to steal and kill and destroy; I have come that they may have life, and have it to the full."*

Philippians 4:8 *"Finally, brothers and sisters, whatever is true, whatever is noble, whatever is right, whatever is pure, whatever is lovely, whatever is admirable—if anything is excellent or praiseworthy—think about such things."*

Reflection

In your view, what is the difference between happiness and joy? Who or what makes you happy? Where does your joy come from? When you are facing difficult times, do you feel happy? Do you still feel joy?

_____

_____

_____

_____

Prayer

Loving God, thank You for the blessings You've so graciously poured over me. I have so many people and things in my life to be thankful for, but I am lacking joy. Happiness abounds in my life and my heart, but I long for the deep sense of your presence and peace so that I may experience never-ending joy. Despite my circumstances, I want to be rooted in your love and have full belief and contentment in your goodness and faithfulness.

Chapter 7: Less Holding On, More Letting Go

As we embark on life's new journeys, we can take comfort in knowing that God is in control.

"Let go and let God." Easier said than done, am I right? Learning how to slow down and let go of how I think things should be is by far the hardest, most challenging practice I learned to face during my season of struggle with anxiety and depression. I had spent my entire adult life white-knuckling my way through each and every day in an attempt to control the unknown. Letting go of my ideas, my plans, my schedule, and my idea of how everything should be was no easy task. And, if I'm being honest, I still struggle with it on a regular basis. Learning to let go was and can be physically and emotionally exhausting, but I have learned that it creates space for me to actually catch my breath and experience the happening, whatever that may be, the way God intended me to experience it. In the process of learning to let go little by little, I have been shown how to live fully alive. I no longer battle the calendar, the clock, and the to-dos ruminating in my mind, which led to me having headaches and shoulder, neck,

> **In the process of learning to let go little by little, I have been shown how to live fully alive.**

and jaw tension. Instead, I have a more trusting way of going through my days; I am surrendered and embracing the journey God has planned for my loved ones and me.

My season of battling insomnia, anxiety, and depression stripped the reigns of control right out of my hands. I lost my grip on the situation when I finally came to the realization that I was not in control—I couldn't fix it by myself, and I couldn't make it go away. I had to relinquish my control. I would give my burden to God many times throughout that yearlong journey, and many times I would take it right back. I am not a patient person, so the fact that I had to wait for answers, wait for doctor appointments, wait for counseling sessions, wait for the medicine to work the way it was made to work…all the waiting was excruciatingly painful for me. But I learned to let go because I knew deep down God was holding on. Learning to let go while I was still struggling with and battling on a daily for my mental health allowed me to see that amidst the struggle, I was also growing and learning how to recognize and accept my own emotions. I was learning to feel my feelings. And most importantly, I was coming to the realization I never had control. I had anxiety. I was living a life that was "thriving" on routine, a strict schedule, predictability,

I was coming to the realization I never had control. I had anxiety.

and comfortable patterns to my days. The problem with this was all of my managing and controlling did not equip me to face the obstacles that come with living life in the real world. Controlling and striving to manage and white-knuckle my way through everything was a naive way to live, and that is why my body had to scream at me. It had to get my attention—hard and fast—because I was living in a make-believe, self-created utopian world. Every day was a mountain of never-ending tasks to be done, controlled, manipulated, and managed by me—all by myself, or at least that was my perception. My days were running together in a blur of ceaseless activity. I ran through them as though I was sprinting to a finish line. But in all reality, that finish line didn't exist, and I was actually limping and crawling my way through my days. I was just too busy to notice it, to accept it, to face it.

One of the most difficult and challenging things for us to do is give over control of our lives to God. This is insanely difficult for us, or at least for me, because we cannot handle when things feel out of our control, even for a minute. We tend to give it, whatever "it" is, to God, and then we try to take it back. We play this game of give it to God, take it back, give it to God, take it back. We often end up messing things up even more, and we can't be used the way God is trying to use us. When we are trying to control all the things, manage all the things, plan all the things- that's the Devil's way of distracting us from seeing God, from hearing God's voice, from listening to God and what He has planned for us. Our minds are overwhelmed and saturated with all of our to-dos, and we lose focus on the most important person that we should be focused on, and that is Jesus.

This was the first time in my entire adult life that I was slowed down. Yes, I was forced. I didn't choose this season. God chose it for me, so I had to sit with myself, my thoughts, my feelings, my wants, desires, passions, and dreams. Up to this point, pre-midlife ~~crisis, mental breakdown,~~ breaking open, I was so busy managing schedules, calendars, and activities, mine and my family's. I was busy meeting the needs, desires, and happiness of others that I never opened up space to focus on myself. I now know I was intentionally busying myself with everyone else's stuff because I was too scared to focus on my own stuff. I mean, who am I? What are my passions? What do I care about? What am I good at (other than running a tight ship and keeping a tidy house)? I stayed busy, doing all the things for all the people, because I didn't want to deal with myself. I didn't want to face my fears, my disappointments, and my degrees of unhappiness. I was living the "too blessed to be stressed" life that society puts on a pedestal. Rather than facing my feelings, I was too busy stuffing them down and hiding them away.

This not knowing myself became so clear to me when my counselor asked me one day, "Who's Jodi? I mean, I know you're Matt's wife, and I know you're a mom and a teacher; I know all the roles you fill because you refer to yourself as those people all the time when we're talking. But, I want you to tell me who YOU are- what are your interests, your dreams, your hobbies? What excites you? What scares you? What lights a fire in your belly? Who are you when you're not fulfilling all the roles you play in other people's lives? I sat there, taken aback—stunned, speechless for several minutes because I didn't know. I didn't have an answer. I wasn't sure who I was, what I liked, or what I would choose to do with myself if I ever had time by myself. I didn't know who I was outside of who I had become for everyone else. I didn't know the Jodi God created for His purpose beyond the roles I played in others' lives. I had forgotten I was chosen by Him, for Him. And that was scary.

I didn't know who I was outside of who I had become for everyone else.

I had forgotten I was chosen by Him, for Him.

Those first few months of counseling did go as I thought they would. I pictured myself lying on a couch, sharing all my fears, and the counselor consoling me and giving me advice and quick tips on how to make it all better and how to make it all go away. But that was not the case. It couldn't have been further from that image. My counselor didn't talk to me, but she did ask a lot of questions. She had a way of making me dig into my own being and examine myself. The sessions consisted of a lot of deep, hard conversations—a lot of questions being asked for me to ponder, reflect, and search deeper in my heart and mind to find "answers." Answers that most likely wouldn't come because there were no clear-cut answers. Nothing I could plan, control, manipulate, or manage. These were matters of the heart, my heart. I can look back now and see how much I grew during that time of weekly sessions with my counselor—sessions of me looking long and hard at myself. I see now that with each session, I was learning how to slow down, take a breath, and examine myself. I was learning how to recognize my feelings, name my feelings, and think about why I was feeling this way. I was learning to be okay with whatever the why was, whatever the feeling was. I learned that I had different feelings on different days, often without explanation, because I am human. I learned that I needed to let go of what I thought my life should be and accept it for what it was—including the fact that I was a wife, mom of four, and a teacher that had to take time away from work to give her own body, mind, and soul some tender loving care. I was learning to see each moment for what it was and letting it be what it needed to be, with no judgment.

Counseling helped me realize that I had lived my life being the person that others thought I should be or needed me to be. When I should have been listening to my own heart and God's words on whom He wanted me to be. By letting go of meeting these expectations, I was able to make room for new thoughts, new feelings, new excitement, and ways of thinking. I saw clearly that I am more than Jodi—the wife, the mom, the teacher, the daughter, the friend—I am me. Yes, I am all those things too, and I love being those things to those people, my people. But, I was not paying enough attention to me. I was, like a lot of adults, losing a sense of myself. While much of my counseling was a struggle, I can now easily see just how much I was growing. Growing into myself and who God intended me to be. By learning to let go of whom I thought I was supposed to be—who I thought others wanted or needed me to be—I became more of who I truly am. I learned that is all anyone else ever wanted from me anyway. I was so busy, so preoccupied, and so worried about pleasing everyone else that I had forgotten how to please myself and how to please God by placing Him first in my life. My roles and my identities with others had become my idols. When I started letting go of trying to be everything to everybody, which no one ever asked me or expected me to be, I did that all to myself—I started to see that I had more time, connection, and true presence with the things and people that

My roles and my identities for and with others had become my idols.

really matter most to me. Most importantly, I made time to be present and connect with God. He became my top priority.

My season of anxiety and depression also led me to live a life more surrendered to Jesus. All those days at home, alone, left me feeling a bit lost, uncertain, and spinning and circles, not knowing what to do. All I had was time. Time to think, time to reflect, time to go to my doctor appointments, time to find myself, and a lot of time to be in God's word and be in prayer for His will and His way to come shining through. As you know, either from just knowing me or reading this far in the book, I have long prided myself on being self-sufficient. This self-sufficiency was the product of a pride-filled life. The self-sufficient mentality. The badge of honor that busyness can bring. It was humbling to experience a season where I had no choice but to surrender to Him and cast all my cares on Him. I had always had the tendency to do everything on my own. This struggle, this dark, scary season, made me realize that I can't do this life on my own. God never intended me to, and I think He was using this struggle, this battle, to show me just how much I need Him. He offered himself up for me and to me and he has blessed me with the gifts of others in my life to walk alongside me. When I hold on to things in my life with my white-knuckling grip of control, it is 100% about my pride. It is about my need to get it all just right to reach perfection. It is the fear of the unknown and our fear of being wrong, messing up, and making mistakes that create most of our angst and anxiety. God taught me. He made me relearn that I need faith and reason to make meaning in this uncertain world. I need Him to make sense of all that doesn't. Something tells me you too need this too. You need Him.

Nothing has shown me my need for God's grace, goodness, and guidance more than being a momma to my four amazing kiddos. In my younger mothering years, I controlled my kids' eating, nap, and play schedules. It then moved to control over their clothes, homework, school projects, sports, play dates, birthday parties, you name it. From there, it moved to trying to control, in vain, their friendships, their screen time, their food choices, their bedtimes, their choice of music, and how they spent their free time. Matt and I also liked to plan in detail (aka control) family trips, vacations, and random fun days. Everything had a plan in our days, just like everything had a place in our house. As you can imagine, this left me, and Matt, feeling worn down, stressed, and exhausted most of the time. We were so busy planning and executing the perfect plan that we often missed out on the moment. We held tight to our kids, our schedules, and our routines as if we could fix anything bad that might happen, or more like keep it from happening in the first place. I used to have the drive and determination to fix anything if I worked a little harder or spent more time pouring and obsessing and worrying over it. But I have learned that some things just aren't meant to be fixed, or at least not fixed by me. Most of the time, in life, we just need to accept things as they are and be at peace with whatever that may be. In all my efforts and ceaseless striving to keep my kids safe from harm, I was doing them harm. It does our kids no good to be a constant rescue and safety net for them. We can only teach them how to rise from falling by letting them fall.

> In all my efforts and ceaseless striving to keep my kids safe from harm, I was doing them harm. It does our kids no good to be a constant rescue and safety net for them. We can only teach them how to rise from falling by letting them fall.

A lot of growth came from my season of struggle for both of us. As Matt realized he couldn't control or fix my anxiety and depression, he learned to release his grip too. Our faith lives grew more in this season than at any other time in our lives. We become closer as husband and wife, and our kids saw firsthand that bad times can hit anyone, anywhere, anytime—no matter how much planning has been done. Up to this point in our lives, none of us, Matt, the kids, or myself, had experienced many struggles or real, deep pain. Our lives had been smooth sailing, so to speak. But this season taught us differently. It taught us we can't avoid the valleys of life by controlling or manipulating the circumstances. We, I'm including you here too, have to shift our mindset to focus on the blessings in the valleys. We are always children of God; He is with us in all of our valleys every bit as much as He is with us on our mountaintops. We just have to be willing to let go of our grasp, stop holding on, and wait and watch for what He wants us, our kids, and our lives to become. He has a plan, our stories are already written by Him. We need to trust and walk in obedience with Him even when we don't feel like it—even when we're scared. Trust the process, friends, trust that the seed has been planted and there is growth happening. Trust that He holds the harvest of our lives. Whether we see it in our lifetime or not, regardless of if we are in the midst of the fight of our lives, we must remember that when the rains come, the valleys fill first. When we stop trying to hold it all together, we can rest in letting it all go into the arms and sovereign love of the God who holds us.

> **When we stop trying to hold it all together, we can rest in letting it all go into the arms and sovereign love of the God who holds us.**

Casting our cares and anxieties on Him because He cares for us is a sign of humility. So let's set aside our self-sufficient, pride-filled ways and humble ourselves before our almighty God. For if we humble ourselves, we will be exalted. Jeremiah 29:11 stands out to me as the verse I found myself clinging to as we embarked on a letting go journey like no other— the sending our firstborn off to college journey. Letting go is important but there is one type of holding on that comes with letting go. Holding on is not controlling my feelings, managing my day, or white-knuckling my circumstances. Holding on is leaning on my faith in God—my trust in His promise that He will provide.

The following is an excerpt from an article I wrote the summer I was preparing my heart and mind to let go of our firstborn, Anna. She was headed to Knoxville to begin her freshman year at the University of Tennessee. There are some additions to this excerpt, as we are now preparing to send our son Jack to college at The University of Cincinnati. God continues to reveal to me that while my heart hurts to see them go, He is holding them so carefully, so closely.

It was her first day of Kindergarten, and Anna, adorned with her adorable back-to-school hairdo, colorful gingham dress, and purple backpack, flashed her excited, "Here I come, World!" smile as she clumsily climbed the stairs onto the big yellow bus. She glanced back for one more wave, her ocean-blue eyes locking in on mine, brimming with tears.

Do you, too, remember your baby's first day of Kindergarten like it was yesterday?

It can't be true that our vivid memories etched ever so clearly in our minds were thirteen years ago. But it is true. It has been thirteen years. And now I, and maybe you too, find myself on the brink of launching my baby into the world as she heads off to her first year of college. The last few months have been bursting with high school graduation happenings, diligent list-making for all things college, and numerous trips to Target and clicks on Amazon.

In the midst of all the hustle, in a quiet moment with God, it dawned on me that I was experiencing the same worries that I had on Anna's first day of Kindergarten. My mind and heart were harboring endless concerns: Is she scared? Will she meet new friends easily? What happens if she gets sick and I'm not there to care for her? Who will hug her when she is sad? Catch her tears when she is lonely? Remind her to get enough sleep?

I was blathering in an attempt to pray the perfect prayer over Anna and myself during this ride of roller-coaster emotions. I was flailing; the words would not come, but the tears were streaming down my cheeks. And then, with one big inhale and exhale, a sense of calm washed over me. I felt the presence of the Holy Spirit reminding me that God is in control. I was released from the self-induced burden of perfect prayer and comforted by the reminder that He is the creator and author of Anna's story. He has blessed us this far in life, so I shouldn't worry that He'd fail us now.

But we must remember they are never truly ours, but they are, have always been, and will always belong to God.

Parenting is one of God's greatest blessings, but it can also elicit our worry and need for prayer the most. Letting them go is so very difficult. But we must remember they are never truly ours, but they are, have always been, and will always belong to God. Our kids are within the loving borders of our nests for only so long. Then they are off, flying on their own, as God intended them to. As parents, we can learn to let go, knowing He is holding on to all of us. This next step is not about God blessing our plans for our kids' lives. It is about us relinquishing con-trol and worry so that we can bear witness to the beautiful story He is sure to tell in and through them.

As parents, we can learn to let go, knowing He is holding on to all of us.

How do we do this-the letting go, the handing over control? How do we assure our kids that everything is going to be okay? Matt and I find ourselves facing this bittersweet moment in life, times two, now that we are launching our son, Jack, out into the world to begin his college journey. I had to learn the hard way and am still learning the old saying, "To never have failed is to never have tried." I am learning to apply this to my own living and to support my kids as they grow, learn, take risks, succeed, fail, and fall. When we haven't experienced a fall or failure of some sort—a season of hardship and pain—we're not complete, we're not whole, because to be human is to have suffered. I had to learn the hard way that in order for me to live a full life, a present life, and rich and joyful life, I had to stop and release my desire to have a handle on everything. I had to surrender my desire to grip tightly and control everything, and I had to give it to God. I had to leave it there—no taking it back.

Well, we draw on our faith, we turn to God's Word, and we remind ourselves and our kids of His promise, "Be strong and courageous. Do not be afraid; do not be discouraged, for the Lord your God will be with you wherever you go" (Joshua 1:9). We help our students view this new chapter of their lives through the lens of God's sovereignty. We trust that He is using this part of their story, all the changes, new firsts, and struggles to mold, train, and equip them for all that He has in store.

Our faithful following of Jesus is the best example we can ever set for our children. Being obedient to God's calling on our lives as their parents, leading them in His way, and reminding them that they are to do His will is how we can lead them to the path of His peace. We can ask God to give us the wisdom we need to release our grip on our children's lives. God gifted them to us; so let's give our children back to Him, trusting that He will do His good works in and through them.

God gifted them to us; so let's give our children back to Him, trusting that He will do His good works in and through them.

As we begin our voyage in uncharted waters, we can take comfort in knowing God is in control. He is the only one that truly knows what is best for our kids and what plans He has for them. This doesn't mean that we are off the hook when it comes to parenting them through this exciting and tumultuous time. This doesn't mean that our kids don't still need us. They do. They still need us; they still want us. And doesn't that feel good?

How can we lovingly support our kids when they are starting to outgrow our daily scheduling and managing everything for them or when they are no longer living with us? When they are no longer under our wings? We can make sure they know they can still ask for help. We can be available to them, listen without criticism or judgment, and give them advice—if and only if they ask for it. We can remind them that they are not trying to fulfill our dreams for them, but they are embarking on their own journey to fulfill their own dreams. We need to remain quiet so they can hear Christ speaking to them through the Holy Spirit. We should constantly remind them that God's plans are bigger than their struggles. They will build courage and resilience if we allow them to flounder a bit. We shouldn't be quick to fix their problems or give them the answers- they need to take risks, accept challenges, and experience failure. Finally, we need to make sure they know we are proud of WHO they are, not WHAT they do.

Remember all the times we wished away? The sleepless nights, nap schedules, potty training, shoe tying, swimming, and bike riding lessons. Remember how endless they seemed? And now, we live the reality of how quickly they passed.

Remember the excitement over all their firsts? Their first word, first step, the first day of Kindergarten, first lost tooth, first sleepover, first time backing out of the driveway on their own. Those firsts came and went, but we'll cherish them forever. So let's get excited and let our hearts be filled with joy thinking of all the glorious firsts God has in store for them in the next four years. "'For I know the plans I have for you,' declares the Lord, 'plans to prosper you and not to harm you, plans to give you hope and a future'" (Jeremiah 29:11).

Saying goodbye or moving on from the first chapter of "firsts" may seem unbearable, but we can hold tight to all the memories. The bitterness that comes with packing up all their belongings as they prepare to leave our nest is also sprinkled with so much sweetness as we watch them spread their wings and fly.

The bitterness that comes with packing up all their belongings as they prepare to leave our nest is also sprinkled with so much sweetness as we watch them spread their wings and fly.

Scripture

Jeremiah 29:11 *"For I know the plans I have for you,' declares the Lord, 'plans to prosper you and not to harm you, plans to give you hope and a future.'"*

Joshua 1:9 *"Have I not commanded you? Be strong and courageous. Do not be afraid; do not be discouraged, for the Lord your God will be with you wherever you go.'"*

Reflection

What is something that you are trying to control and manage in your life right now? How is that affecting your heart? Your happiness? Your anxiety? Your joy? Your sleep? Do you find yourself white-knuckling your way through your days to maintain a sense of "control"? How does that make you feel (physically, mentally, emotionally) by the end of the day? How can you begin your day in a more surrendered "letting go" approach? What might go awry if you "let go"? What's the worst that could happen?

_____

_____

_____

_____

Prayer

Dear God, In this moment, I want to let go of all my thoughts and concerns. I know when I let go, I will be able to receive your goodness and love. When my hands are formed into tight fists, I cannot open my hands to receive any of the blessings you so lovingly and lavishly offer. I want to let go so I can receive your gifts. I know if I let go, I will receive your unending peace in my mind and in my heart. Help me to let go of my desires and my control so that I may receive courage, wisdom, and discernment from you. When I let go, if I fall, I know you will catch me.

Chapter 8: Less Fitting In, More Belonging

When we busy ourselves trying to be like everyone else,
we forget to be more like Him.

I am going to go out on a limb here and assume that you, like me, crave human interaction and connection. I would venture to guess that most humans do. Feeling connected and knowing that we have "our people" is just as much a basic need for us to survive as food and water.

As a teenager, I went above and beyond trying to avoid standing out. And, if you're being honest with yourself, I bet you did too. Standing out in the crowd is not something most teens long for. At all. As is common for most teens, I would say anything, wear anything and do *almost* anything in order to fit in. As an immature, inexperienced being walking around in my own awkward skin, I did not understand what it meant to belong. I followed the crowd and found happiness in just being part of the group no need for belonging, all I wanted was to fit in. Even if deep down I knew what was happening and, in the end, it just made me feel different and more alone in more ways than actually feeling as if I had true friendships and connections. My middle and high school years were all about fitting in and yet feeling so isolated and lonely. But that describes the life of most teenagers, I guess.

We live in a world where people still place a high value on fitting in. This weak attempt at making real connections finds us in our middle and high school years, and even college and beyond is mostly spent trying not to stand out. Just blend in and be like everyone else. The problem with this is that we so desperately want to fit in that we often lose a lot of who we truly are. We become reassured by the familiar. We are comfortable here even if we don't truly belong. The friendships we've made, the group we're a part of, it's all easy, comfortable. So we stay here, and we often find ourselves stuck. The thought of taking a brave step, going off on a different path to seek new adventures, is unfamiliar and scary. There is too much uncertainty.

Often, in order for us to take these big, brave, adventurous new steps, we have to be forced. Maybe we're forced by life circumstances, a season of pain and struggling, or by God Himself. But these brave steps, these leaps of faith, often come as a result of our efforts to simply fit in.

> **He created us to stand out-stand out for ourselves, stand out in a world gone wrong in so many ways, and stand out for Him.**

But friend, we must remember that God did not create us just to fit in. He created us to stand out—stand out for ourselves, stand out in a world gone wrong in so many ways, and stand out for Him. By trying to be like everyone else, we slip away and become no one. We don't need a permission slip to be ourselves. We lose ourselves when we strive to be like everyone else, to please everyone else, to impress everyone else. We slip away from whom God intended us to be. When we're busy trying our best to be like everyone else, we forget to be more like Him. This is the path I found myself on a handful of years ago, and it led me further away from God and straight to physical, emotional, mental, and spiritual exhaustion.

As I continued living my life to be like everyone else, fit in, and just blend with the crowd, I was moving further away from my root life–my relationship with myself and with God. I was becoming more and more self-sufficient at starting friendships and relationships, growing them, and keeping them. But, I was growing away from God and my faith; that part of me was becoming more complacent, more stagnant.

As I've shared, throughout my middle and high school years—and a better part of my college years—I was managing people's perceptions of me rather than showing up as my true self. And to be honest, I carried a lot of this perform and please mentality into my early years of teaching and being a mom. I would walk into a work meeting, a party, a gathering of moms at a school event, you name it, I read the room and shape-formed myself to fit right in. It was an exhausting way to live–constantly switching gears from school Jodi to neighborhood Jodi, to college girls' night Jodi, to church group Jodi, to Mom mode Jodi. I could read the room and fit right in, but when I left the room, I was worn out. Throughout my learning to surrender more, I have learned that being vulnerable and showing who I am right here, right now, in this very moment, is so much simpler than forcing myself to be who I think I am supposed to be or who I think others want me to be. In his book *The Power of Now*, Eckhart Tolle states, "In surrender, you no longer need ego defenses and false masks. You become very simple, very real." [1] That is vulnerability, and vulnerability leads us to true self-discovery.

> That is vulnerability, and vulnerability leads us to true self-discovery.

The fitting-in mentality I was forcing myself to live in was nothing more than assessing and adjusting. Assessing the who's, the what's, the where's, and the how's in order to determine how I showed up. It was a constant shapeshift to match the world around me. Belonging is the exact opposite and I learned that the hard way. After years of striving, pleasing, perfecting, and performing, all on my own, outside of God's will per se, He brought me to a halt so I would be forced to step back, assess, and adjust my way of living. One of the first things He showed me was that most of the people I was performing for, or shapeshifting to fit in with, loved and accepted me for me. There was never a need for me to read the room and fit in. I already belonged. I didn't need to act, think, or do a certain way. I didn't need to earn their approval, they accepted me for me. Another thing God showed me was that the relationships I was trying to keep afloat because I thought I needed them, the ones that were causing me the most anxiety, the most dread, and the most exhaustion, were the relationships I didn't really need. They were not relationships or friendships that He intended to be an integral part of my life. He taught me the difference between acquaintances and true friendships and that I didn't have to pour my heart and soul into every encounter or acquaintance. I learned to embrace who I was, adjusted my lifestyle, and valued friendships accordingly. I stopped shrinking my personality and my drive to pour so much time and energy into friendships that were more about fitting in.

My season of insomnia, anxiety, and depression healed me in many ways. One of the most valuable lessons I learned during the healing process of this difficult time was that people's thoughts about me are just that. They are their thoughts. They are not facts, they are not truths, they are not lies, they are just the thoughts that someone else is having about me. And I am not defined by others' thoughts. And neither are you. My therapist also helped me learn that it is not my job to be likable. There will be people who fall completely and madly in love with me, people who can't stand to be in the same room as me, and people between the two. She reminded me often that my job was to discover myself and be myself, and the right people would be drawn to me for me. That was a big one for me. I had spent most of my years so wrapped up in looking good to myself and others that it was all I really thought or cared about. Now that I have gone through the

> **My therapist also helped me learn that it is not my job to be likable. She reminded me often that my job was to discover myself and be myself, and the right people would be drawn to me for me.**

struggle, the season of pain, and I have grown, learned, and unlearned, and I am in a new season and stage of life, all I care about is looking good for God. Pleasing Him, doing His work, following His calling on my life, and loving whom He has made me to be. I am more confident in who I am—who God made me to be—now than at any other time in my life. He used pain and trials of testing to change me, to make me into this new love-God-first self. In turning to Him, trusting Him, and loving Him first, I can see the transformation in myself. I am growing into myself, my interests, my desires, and my passions. And I am beginning to belong to myself rather than wearing myself out trying to fit in with others.

When God placed me in the fire amidst night after night of insomnia and crippling anxiety, He was taking me on a journey of healing and recovery. He was renewing me and refining me. He was using evil for His good. And while I would never wish what I went through on anyone, I am grateful God carried me through that storm because it has brought me to who I am today. And, boy, do I love her!

When I had to take time off from work to seek counseling and medical attention, I learned that boundaries are a good, healthy, and important thing for us to have in place. In the midst of doing the hard work to help myself heal, I had to set boundaries. I had to set boundaries with my work, my volunteer time, my family, and my friends. I had to step back completely and admit I needed rest. I needed help; I needed to be cared for. This asking for help is the hardest thing I have ever done. But I also know it is the bravest thing I have ever done. Leaning into this season with God, relying on Him, and putting all my faith and trust in Him have taught me how to approach daily callings in my life. I have learned to do what He calls me to do—the hard, the good, the unwanted, the unbelievable because I know it's the right thing. Whatever

Whatever He calls me to, regardless of the attention, praise, approval, or accolades from others, is the right thing.

He calls me to, regardless of the attention, praise, approval, or accolades from others, is the right thing.

When I was in the throes of fitting in and doing what others wanted me to do, I would react out of insecurity. I was in a constant state of alertness, ready to react. I never settled or was in a place to reflect and respond. It was a constant reaction to whatever was happening around me. I have learned that I need to be sure of Him and His promised security. You need to learn this too. When we are insecure, our words and our actions don't align with who we are at our roots. We stray, we falter, and we fake our way through. When we don't lean on Him and turn to Him to show us our way, we will be more easily persuaded and misled. All of our perfecting and performing to please others and to make sure we fit in makes things seem "off". We never feel at peace within ourselves.

Many of us care what others think. And it's okay to care. We do more harm than good to ourselves if we pretend we don't care. But our sense of self-worth has to shift from external–it's me, it's who I am, it's how others see me, think of me, judge me–to whom God created us to be, whom He wants us to be. The world wants us to feel needy. Society wants us to need the approval of others. We are sold cultural fixes for everything from anti-aging skincare routines to outlandish diet and exercise programs. When we are healing from painful seasons, it's important that we not just acknowledge our suffering but seek to be restored. We need to not just focus on what has happened to us but we need to focus on why it happened and how God is using it to change us. We need to look up to Him. He is the ultimate healer, the great physician. He makes all things new.

The learning, and more importantly, the unlearning, I did while growing through my yearlong battle helped me realize that life is less about fitting in all the things. It's less about all the to-dos and accomplishments, the events and jam-packed calendars, and more about being together. I learned that what I needed more than anything was to learn how to be. How to be with myself, my family, my friends, my thoughts. I have learned that it is important to embed ourselves in a circle of friends and family who get us just the way we are and who celebrate and honor us and our journeys—good, bad, and hard. Instead of worrying and obsessing over impressing those we don't even know or care much about, we need to slow down, acknowledge and appreciate the beauty and joy of being with those who lift us up. I now realize that how I feel when I leave a social encounter is truth-telling to how much I should pour into and prioritize that relationship. If I am drained and feel I need to withdraw in order to bounce back from the time spent with that person(s), then that is a huge red flag that I need to let that relationship sail. If, on the other hand, I walk away from that time and encounter feeling energized, uplifted, awakened, and full of joy, then I know that those are the people that I want (need) to spend more time with—time wanting to be more and do less.

I heard Lisa Whittle on a podcast explain that if we find ourselves in a space where we are constantly being marginalized and not let in, and we feel like it is an ongoing sabotage, we don't need to continue to try to ask to be included there as there's a big difference between being tolerated in a room and being invited in and welcomed.[2] Whittle encouraged her listeners not to assess this with unrealistic demands or a selfish spirit but to see it as a space that we need to make sure we should be investing in as a child of God, and if we're constantly coming up against a brick wall and we sense that resistance all the time, then it's probably not the right place or friendship for us because God has gifts that He wants us to use and people that will love us and walk through life with us. We need to seek Him to lead us to those right places. I have learned to accept my emotional wiring and personality—I am an extroverted introvert. That is, I am relational. I love being with people, going places, and experiencing all that life has to offer. But, but, but.... I don't have the bandwidth, headspace, or capacity that others may have. My social battery depletes quickly. I enjoy a night out with my family, friends, or coworkers, but then I immediately need time to myself. I need quiet, solitude, and stillness. I used to loathe this about myself. Not anymore.

> **True belonging means we give up the need to please everyone all the time. We become comfortable and at peace with disappointing others.**

It's now one of the things I love most about myself because I recognize what I need, and I give it to myself unapologetically.

Along with laying down my incessant need to be a part of all things social, the need to be "friends" with everyone, and fitting in with all the circles, my spiritual awakening has also taught me that it's important for me to belong to myself, to make peace with myself. After all, I can't belong to others if I don't first belong to Him and second to myself. True belonging means we give up the need to please everyone all the time. We become comfortable and at peace with disappointing others. Because let's face it, if we honor God first and then ourselves, we will always disappoint someone, and disappointing others was not something I was willing to do. This pressure to be and do all things for all the people in my life was not a pressure anyone put on me. I did that all by myself. I did it to myself. Matt and our kids never demanded or expected me to perform or perfect all the happenings in our day-to-day lives. And my coworkers certainly didn't demand anything out of me or from me. But I felt that need, and I put that pressure on myself. So when God brought me to my knees in the summer of 2017, I had no choice but to stop and focus on myself. I had to learn how to focus on myself—how to recognize and accept my feelings—good and bad. How to slow down, ease up, and even let go of all the things. God did not undo me so that He could show me how to focus on myself and stay there. No, he undid me so that I could become self-focused for a time in order to show up more effectively and authentically for those in my life. I felt like I was disappointing my family, friends, and coworkers, but I had to pull back in order to care for myself—in order to rest, seek medical treatment, and find myself.

The more I made peace with myself by getting over the fear of disappointing others, the more I realized I could stop bending myself into contortions to appear as if I always had it all together. I am more willing to show up as my true, raw, authentic self because

I now realize that honoring my limitations, preferences, and needs is not self-resignation; it's an active process of understanding where I am currently and accepting that in tension with where I want to be.

I am staying honest with myself and God. I now realize that honoring my limitations, preferences, and needs is not self-resignation; it's an active process of understanding where I am currently and accepting that in tension with where I want to be. I'm at peace because I know, God knows, and others know. I'm not wasting precious energy pretending or hiding. It has taken me a long time to acknowledge and accept my anxiety. I always knew it was there, but I didn't want it to be because it made me feel less than others. But now, I feel my anxiety, I accept it, and I remind myself that it's not going to take over. It can be with me for the ride, but it's not driving. I will not let it take the wheel. Instead, I invite God in with my fears and anxiety. So if we want to take brave steps to heal, to grow, and to become all God created us to be, we have to learn to stop over-committing and overextending ourselves in order to please others. Just like I learned not to let my anxiety take over, I no longer let all the other players have their way with me. I don't feel the need to justify or make excuses for any of my feelings. I just notice them, and I am honest with myself and God (and others—I don't give an every "How are you?" or "How's your day?" a fake "I'm good, everything's great" response). I live with both the presence of who I am and the rough spots I have.

When I make peace with myself and all the thoughts, feelings, emotions, and reactions I have in my mind and my body, I begin to notice the presence of a new friend, a new belonging…me. I am finding myself to be more enjoyable to spend time with. I am beginning to discover a sense of safety within myself. I no longer fear the parts that have gotten the best of me in the past—the parts that caused me to lash out, to envy, to perform, to control, or to spiral out into anxiety. I am learning that I am my own best friend. There is no more shaming or beating myself up. To live at peace with others means I must be faithful to myself. I don't want to betray myself. I know myself, I enjoy myself, I understand myself, and I want to treat myself kindly. Living at peace with others means paying attention to what I need to stay healthy in my relationships. I know you want this for yourself too. This may mean that we change and grow alongside someone, or it may mean we stay distant from those who can't respect or honor our boundaries. We are conditioned to place our self-worth on how well we make others feel, but

> **Remember that Jesus disappointed people. He didn't always act the way His followers wanted. He wasn't selfish, but he operated out of integrity.**

I have learned that we need to measure our self-worth by living from our own integrity. We need to balance our responsibility to others with our responsibility to our God-given self.

Remember this: Jesus disappointed people. He didn't always act the way his followers wanted. He wasn't selfish, but he operated out of integrity. So, when we feel that pull on our minds and that tug at our heart to act, do, or say something that others want us to, all for the sake of fitting in, we must remember Jesus' example. We must focus on what God wants, not what others want. We must stay true to our calling and try our very best not to focus on temporary, worldly distractions. Being a follower of Christ comes at a cost. As we partner with God, we will inevitably disappoint others. As Jesus told his disciples in Matthew 16:24-26, "Whoever wants to be my disciple must deny themselves and take up their cross and follow me. For whoever wants to save their life will lose it, but whoever loses their life for me will find it. What good will it be for someone to gain the whole world yet forfeit their soul? Or what can anyone give in exchange for their soul?" A person that comes to mind when I think of living with integrity and humility is my dad. My dad was the same person, no matter where he was or who he was with. He always said and did what he felt and knew to be right in his heart, regardless of what others might think or how they might respond. I used to think that was a trait that came with age and wisdom. As I have the privilege to age, I see this to be true.

The older I get, the less consumed I am with impressing others and saying and doing all the "right" things in an effort to fit in. Living with integrity comes with putting on a coat of humility. Living on this earth into my late 40s and experiencing more people, more societal advancements, adjustments, and changes, and going through strenuous seasons of learning and unlearning has taught me the one thing that's most important. It's not about me. It's just not. My life, my relationships, my failures, my successes, my experiences, and my adventures—none of them are about me. They are about me living a life that points others to Jesus. They are about me glorifying, praising, and honoring Him in all I say and do. Do I fall short in this area? Yes. Every single day. But I know that He sees my heart, He knows my intentions, and His mercies are new to me every morning. Also, falling short just shows people that, as a Christian, I have struggles and bad days too. Yet, they see me get back up and try again and they notice I make my life about growing closer to God, building his Kingdom,

> **Whether or not I "fit in" truly does not matter because when it comes to the family of God, we all fit in. We all belong.**

and belonging to a family of believers. Whether or not I "fit in" truly does not matter because when it comes to the family of God, we all fit in. We all belong. Ephesians 2:13 tells us, "But now in Christ Jesus, you who once were far away have been brought near by the blood of Christ." There is no worry or wasted effort over trying to fit in with the family of God. We all belong because of Jesus' sacrifice for us on the cross.

As we learn to live a life rooted in Christ, we grow, heal, and change our patterns of behavior, and we grow closer to God and become more fully who He wants us to be. We've all had times in our lives when we have been rejected, when our friends misunderstood us, or even when those we thought were friends turned their backs on us. Jesus, when He took on the sins of the world, felt abandoned and rejected too. Yet, His rejection was the road that led our sins to be forgiven, and by this forgiveness, we can be adopted into God's family. Jesus's sacrifice and death on the cross for our sins have redeemed us from rejection. God's perfect love replaces our fears of rejection and our hurt of not fitting in. He comforts us and assures us of our belonging with Him. When we experience this transformation, we may not fit in with everyone as we once did. This doesn't mean that we've done something wrong. It simply means we are living with more integrity and humility. We are living out of God's will, not our own. It's not about us anymore. It's all about Him. As I live at peace with myself and face the fear of disappointing others, I gain humility. I see myself in the enormity of this universe He has created, and I accept my God-given limitations. I no longer live to satisfy myself or others, and I don't try to impress God by making sacrifices or wearing myself out overdoing all the things. I try my best to live the life God has chosen for me. The story of Saul in 1 Samuel is the story of someone who rationalizes and explains away their own sin. Saul was God's chosen king over Israel, yet he disobeyed God and followed his own desires. And Samuel said, "Does the Lord delight in burnt offerings and sacrifices as much as in obeying the Lord? To obey is better than sacrifice, and to heed is better than the fat of rams" (1 Samuel 15:22). We can release the burden of performing to fit in and know that our belonging is with Christ if we follow His way for us. When we obey God's calling on our lives, when we show up with honor, love, and intentionality, we are equipped to show up more effectively for others. Living this way loosens us from the stranglehold of expecting ourselves to meet every need around us because they are not all our call to serve.

God can and will give us the courage to stop living our lives to please others. We need to have confidence in who we are and who He has made us to be. We need to show up as our true selves. God can give us wisdom and discernment on how we can live at peace with others without betraying ourselves. Our lives are far too precious and short to spend all of our time trying to please others. If we find ourselves spending a lot of energy and time in an effort to "get along" with someone, it may just be God's way of telling us to step away from the relationship. Maybe this person is draining or is not someone God wants us to spend time with. Maybe their values aren't the same as ours, or maybe we find ourselves compromising who we are at our core when we are with them. We can spend our lives trying to be who everyone wants us to be or who we think we're supposed to be, but we will never be happy. We will never be free. So why don't we all do ourselves a huge favor and just be the true, real us God made us to be? We don't need permission from anyone to be who we already are.

Scripture

Romans 12:5 *"So in Christ we, though many, form one body, and each member belongs to all the others."*

Galatians 6:10 *"Therefore, as we have an opportunity, let us do good to all people, especially to those who belong to the family of believers."*

Isaiah 43:1 *"But now, this is what the Lord says—*
he who created you, Jacob,
he who formed you, Israel:
'Do not fear, for I have redeemed you;
I have summoned you by name; you are mine.'"

Reflection

How would you describe the difference between fitting in and belonging? Write about a time when you worked really hard to fit in. How did it make you feel? With whom or where do you feel you truly belong?

_____

_____

_____

_____

Prayer

Heavenly Father, one of my deepest desires is to have a sense of belonging. At times, my desire to fit in, to be accepted, and to be liked, I have sacrificed my authenticity and, at times, my integrity in order to feel as if I belonged. Lord, help me to experience and value the kinds of deep connections that you created me to have. Give me the strength and courage to know that you are always with me regardless of anyone here on earth that may reject me. Thank you for inviting me into an eternal life with you where I will always be wanted, desired, known, accepted, and loved.

Chapter 9: Less of Me, More of Him

We must realize that our worth is in and from God,
not in what we do or produce.

As I have shared in the previous chapters, my season of pain and relentless struggle with insomnia, anxiety, and depression taught and grew me in so many ways. My journey was one of hard work, effort, determination, trust, and letting go. As I learned to do less and lay down my nature of performing, pleasing, and perfecting, I was able to release the constant need I had to do all the things for all the people. What I hadn't completely surrendered, though, was my thinking that I was still in charge. I was the one that was healing myself; I was seeking, searching, finding, and getting the help I needed. I was the one making decisions that would lighten my load and give me time just to be—time to escape the constant doing, time to rest and heal. For a brief stint, I naively thought I was controlling the path of my being whole again. My getting well was on me. I carried the weight on my shoulders, and it was my cross to bear.

But what I soon discovered rather early on in my healing journey was that in order for me to be well and to feel whole again, I had to surrender my illusion of control and certainty because there is only one thing or person that is for certain, and that is Jesus. God is in control,

> **I had to be open to the realization that my suffering was not exempting me from God's work.**

and He has my best interest at heart. I had to be open to the realization that my suffering was not exempting me from God's work. As I faced my uphill, relentless battle, it was so easy for me to turn inward and find ways to numb and hide my pain. For the longest time, as I faced this battle, I was turning to my comfortable ways of controlling and resisting instead of allowing God to refine me. I was getting wrapped up in the fix it now, fix it fast mode, and I was missing the work—the restoring, refining, and renewing—God was doing in me.

> **I was getting wrapped up in the fix it now, fix it fast mode, and I was missing the work-the restoring, refining, and renewing-God was doing in me.**

I can see it all so clearly now. Now that I am through the fire and have experienced real growth and healing, I can see the work God was, and still is, doing in and through me. But the me that was in the midst of the fire, the me that was being consumed by the flames, couldn't see the beauty that was being born from the ashes. A memory from the early days of my struggle is singed in my mind. It was a summer morning, and I was sitting outside in the quiet, still dark, early morning hours—my chest constricting in and out and my shoulders bobbing up and down, almost uncontrollably, from my sobs. I sensed someone coming up behind me. My back was to the door, so I could look out into our backyard surroundings as I was searching for joy in the beauty of the summer flowers, the songs of the birds, and the anticipating of warmth that the rising sun would hopefully cast on me. Matt approached me. "Good morning, love," he said as he tenderly placed his hands on my shoulders and began to rub them and my neck. "Did you get any sleep at all last night?" Unable to hold the gasps and force of tears, I turned and glanced his way, my tired, sad, hopeless eyes meeting his. "No, I didn't." I went on to share with him that all I felt I could do was lay awake, worry, and wonder why this was happening to me, what was happening to me, and how much longer it was it going to last. I was nearing my breaking point–I was beginning to feel that I could not endure sleepless nights and plodding through my days exhausted, scared, and overwhelmingly alone.

I started having sleepless nights about a month before that particular morning. That morning where I shared with Matt that I was scared, that I felt like a shell of myself, and that I was tired of trying to hide my sadness, my exhaustion, and my feelings of loneliness and despair from the kids. I started going outside each morning so that my sobs wouldn't wake the kids or rouse our Max, who is always keenly aware when something is not right with one of us. I felt at this time that the only thing I could control, the only thing I had the energy to do, was seek God. I didn't pray beautiful prayers or lay my requests confidently at His feet. I didn't have the energy, stamina, or mental capacity to know what to ask for. All I did was sit with tears streaming down my face, my head rested on folded hands, and I pleaded to God for help. I didn't know what to ask for because I didn't know what was wrong with me. I was ashamed that I was so lost, so out of it, in such despair that I felt like a desperate child in need of His fixing of me.

My mind was scattered, I was in such a fog that I would read Scripture, and in the midst of reading, I would draw blanks on what He was trying to say to me. Five minutes after spending time with Him, I would not recall His promises. I aimlessly wondered about our house all day, shuffling from room to room—trying to find hiding places to close my eyes and, more often than not, weep. I was clinging, holding on, to a point where I knew that what I was going through was beyond my control, out of my reach of fixing. As I sluggishly traversed the terrain that was my norm that summer of 2017, I was still trying to solve my own problems and fix whatever it was that was wrong with me. I knew I felt anxious, which in turn was robbing me of sleep. And scarier, to me, was how tired and depressed I was feeling.

I am, or I was, a self-proclaimed control freak. I schedule things, I fix things, I manage things, and I keep all the plates spinning and all the things moving forward. This is where my pride enters stage left. Being in charge and managing all the people and all the things leads to me not having the ability to trust someone else–admittedly, shamefully at times, even God. I have always been a believer, but my belief was on my terms. As long as things were going my way, as long as everyone was happy, everything looked nice, and my sailing was smooth–I was all in on God and trusted Him completely. Looking back over the course of my life and especially over my season of struggling with my mental health, I see that I wanted to be driving the car, and I was letting God ride shotgun. I would hand a problem, concern, or issue over to God, and when it wasn't working out the way I wanted it to or not as fast as I felt it should, I would take it right back into my white-knuckle-controlling grip. The problem with this, and it is a lesson I learned the hard way, is that I needed to give the wheel to Jesus and leave it in His hands.

This sudden onslaught of no sleep, weepy days, and an overall withdrawal from who I had always been was hard. I had no desire to be out and about doing all the normal, fun summer activities. All I wanted to do was sit down, lie down, and rest. But my mind was racing; I couldn't sit still, and I spent most of my days dreading going to bed that night as I worried over whether or not I would sleep. This was such a difficult time for me, and I know it was hard on Matt to see me going through this and knowing there was nothing he could do for me—he's a fixer too. I didn't want the kids to worry about me or see me sad. This was their summer break, a time for them to kick back, take a break from the demands of school, and have fun. But I was anything but fun. I wasn't happy. I was sad, and deep down, I knew they knew that. They saw it in my forced smiles, my sudden drastic weight loss, and my lack of energy and zest for life.

Due to the daily hard grind, it was so difficult for me to see how God might be working. I wanted to be strong in my faith and honorable in my suffering. I wanted to believe that He was using it all for good, and

I knew He didn't want me to hide in my suffering. Deep down, I knew, and I pleaded with Him in prayer. "God, if you are using this so that I can help someone in the future, I will gladly bear this cross." I was trying my best to show my family and friends that I was still trusting in my good God, even during this trial. But it was hard. I found myself clinging in desperation to my knowledge of who Jesus is and who He had always been in my life. I had to let go of my struggle and the idea that it was a battle for me to fight. I had to meet Jesus in the midst of my pain. He put me in the center of this fire so that I would find Him and remain in Him. He was teaching me, *and still is*, that He did not create me to perform, produce, fix, or fight. He created me to trust and remain in Him. I needed to restore my ability to trust Him in the unknown, in the dark, in the hard and scary parts of my story. He was teaching me that my faith and trust in Him, my willingness to surrender and allow Him to work in and through me, would take me further in life that all my hustle ever could or will.

> He was teaching me, and still is, that He did not create me to perform, produce, fix, or fight. He created me to trust and remain in Him.

> He was teaching me that my faith and trust in Him, my willingness to surrender and allow Him to work in and through me, would take me further in life than all my hustle ever could or will.

I know now that while I felt nothing but sheer overwhelm and exhaustion, Jesus was giving me everything I needed to survive each day—manna. I so badly wanted my circumstances to change, so I wouldn't have to keep facing these grueling days. But Romans 5:3-4 reminded me, "... but we also glory in our sufferings, because we know that suffering produces perseverance; perseverance, character; and character, hope." I was clinging to this hope when in October of that same year, I was still suffering in many and mighty ways, and I had to take time off work in order to begin the actual healing process. My time at home left me alone in the quiet, empty house. And I now know this is exactly what I needed. God always knew, but I sure didn't. In fact, at first, I was terrified to be home by myself. I was fearful I might do something to harm myself. While Max, our lab, kept me company and poured his unconditional love all over me, all I had all those days was God. And because the house was so quiet—Matt was at work, and the kids were at school—I began to hear God's voice. No, I didn't hear an actual audible voice, but I could sense His presence and hear Him speaking to me through his written word. I was inhaling my Bible, searching desperately for answers and hope. And I found it.

God's written word, His living word, comforted me, brought me peace, and left me feeling hopeful in Him despite my desperate situation. Jesus enveloped me, and I continued to dig deep into His promises. Looking back, I know God had to bring me to my knees; he had to put a full stop to my body and mind in order to get my attention. I admit that had I not taken time off work to get the help I needed, I would not have heard from God in the way in which I did. He needed and wanted me—just me—to be consumed with Him, with no distractions, barriers, or to-do lists. Just me and Jesus. He needed me to be at home with nothing to do so my sense of self-worth could shift from external worldly factors to me and Him. My perspective needed to switch from who I am to whom God created me to be. Just me and Jesus.

The Book of Romans became an anchor for my drowning soul. I found myself praying verses out loud, I would recite them in the shower, I would write them in my journal, I would use them as the guide for my breath prayers, and I would take prayer walks repeating these verses over and over. I found Romans 12:12 to be extremely comforting. "Be joyful in hope, patient in affliction, faithful in prayer." This was my personal mantra to carry on and remain faithful in my fight. I kept telling myself, "Jodi, this is happening for a reason; whatever it is, God will see you through." A huge motivator for me then and now is to think about how God might use my struggle and pain to help someone else. Maybe my suffering was or will be for someone else's salvation. I thought maybe He was, but now I know He is, teaching, refining, and equipping me in ways that I would, in turn, use to extend my hand and help someone else. Knowing that God was using my trial to teach me, to teach others, to help me or someone else grow—knowing that my pain and suffering are not just for my own growth, helped me to keep going, to keep enduring and persevering, and to do so with patience. I was so overcome with anxiety and depression that I learned to set aside my selfish ways, my plans, and my master calendar manipulation and surrender to Him— time in prayer with Him and His word. I began to desire and crave Him more than anything else. I slowly began to realize that He was all I had, and He was all I needed. Yes, I had the love of my husband, kids, family, and friends, but none of them could carry my grief, take away my pain, or fill me with hope like God.

I had forgotten that every aspect of my life is important, including my spiritual self. I wasn't focused on keeping God in all of it. I had my work life - I nailed that job day in and day out. I had my family life- I managed that with the love, support, and help of Matt. I had my friendships - I kept all that up and running even if, and when I was running ragged. I had my exercise life - I was killing that, too, with early morning workouts. I was prioritizing all the ways of living—physical, relational, and emotional over the most important part of my well-being—my spiritual connection to God. I lost sight of the fact that "He is before all things, and in Him, all things hold together" (Colossians 1:17). I was nourishing my body by exercising, drinking water, and eating well, and I was taking care of my relational needs by loving my family well, keeping in close contact with friends, and investing in meaningful relationships, but I was not prioritizing my spiritual life. My rushed prayers, weekly Sunday stop at church, and half-hearted connection with God were causing me to run on empty. He cares about all of me, but I wasn't prioritizing Him. He was getting my leftovers. I needed a wake-up call that went beyond "I've got this. I'm fine. Everything's fine." I needed Him. I thought I could do everything in my own strength, but God was showing me that He made me to be all that I am through Him- His truth, His word.

Even though I was in the depths of darkness and despair, I was able to continue to trust in the word that is Jesus- even if I was in the dark. His light kept shining through. I may not have felt His loving presence at every moment of those dark days, and I will be the first to admit that I questioned Him, I doubted Him, I shook my fists at Him and cried, "Why are you doing this to me?" But when I look back on those days, I know He was there every step of the way, and He wasn't just talking to

> **But when I look back on those days, I know He was there every step of the way, and He wasn't just talking to me or holding my hand-He was carrying me.**

me or holding my hand—He was carrying me. He was sheltering me in His loving arms. I was able to withstand that horrible, rough patch of life because my God was standing with me. He was teaching me, shaping me, changing me. He was using this season to show me that there is more to life than striving, manipulating, managing, and controlling. There is actually free living in Him and with Him. He taught me the importance of prioritizing Him, starting and ending my days with my mind and thoughts on Him, how He shows up for my family and me, and how He makes the dull, mundane, ordinary life extraordinary. He taught me the beauty of being fully human by reminding me that He, too, became human and walked this earth. He enjoyed slowing down, resting, and having meals with loved ones. He, too, was tired, frustrated, and disappointed by injustices. His work in me was to show me my body, my mind, and, more importantly, my soul were longing for these things— the stopping, the slowing down, the living of life.

I look back and see that while I didn't feel qualified or strong enough to tackle those days, I was because of Him. His strength in me is what got me through. And on those days when I felt He was punishing me, or I wondered how a loving God would let this happen to me, I was comforted by knowing He loves me and He loves those of us that are

> **There is suffering and heartache, but God uses the very things He hates in order to accomplish what He loves.**

disciples for Him. He was using this trial in my life so that he could teach me and help others. He was carrying me through this struggle so that I would draw closer to Him. We have to realize that it is bad in this world. There is suffering and heartache, but God uses the very things He hates in order to accomplish what He loves. My struggle with anxiety and depression taught me the importance of making Him the first priority in my life. And through that relationship with Him, I now know the importance of shining light on mental and spiritual health, and I am prayerful that what I share, what I say, and what I write points others to Him.

As I learned to lean more on God, I learned that I can lean on and count on others too. I must share my gifts because by doing so, I am sharing Him. I learned that I am more than just a wife, a mom, a daughter, a sister, a teacher, or a friend. He reminded me that I am His daughter, and He is using me to build His Kingdom. He showed me that by fulfilling my most important role— living a life surrendered to Him— that I would be all that He wanted me to be. The world doesn't need more people with more titles. The world needs more people loving God, loving others, and loving themselves.

> **The world doesn't need more people with more titles. The world needs more people loving God, loving others, and loving themselves.**

As I came out of my season of anxiety and depression and began to see the light again, the one thing that was crystal clear to me was God— His love, His provision, His grace, and His mercies. I realized that while I was in the moment, the daily seeking and actively pursuing Him every morning was a rope I was grasping for, but now it is my lifeline. Just as John the Baptist realized his purpose in this world was to exalt Christ, not himself. I, too, learned the invaluable lesson, "He must become greater; I must become less" (John 3:30). Through God's great work in me, I learned, and am still learning, that doing less—less striving, less pleasing, less perfecting, and less performing—allows God to do so much more. I now wake every morning with a desire to commune with Him. I start and end every day talking to and listening to Him. What was once a life preserver has become my life. Just because Jesus is Lord, He only becomes Lord of your life when you allow Him to do so. By allowing Him to be the Lord of our lives, we are allowing Him to become greater. I share my story, hoping it points others straight to Jesus. I hope people will ask questions, and I can share Him with them. I have had a few women reach out to me for support and guidance in their own mental health struggles. They thank me for being open, honest, and for vulnerably sharing my story. And while I am happy that my story is able to help them through their mental health struggles, I am overjoyed that I have the opportunity to share my faith, my God, with them.

I have come to learn that if I shift my focus to the one thing that matters most in this life–Jesus– and if I become less and I allow Him to become greater, then my life will be richer and fuller.

By living a life that is less about me and more about Him, a life filled with more humility, I am living the fullest, most content life I could ever imagine. Jesus taught us about humility from the moment of His birth. He was born in the humblest of circumstances. He was God and yet he chose to come to earth as a human. And out of His great love for us, He even chose to obey God to the point of dying a criminal's painful death on the cross for our sins. He's never too busy to listen to me, to help me, to guide me through my struggles and worries. He gladly, with open arms, meets me every morning and He soothes me to sleep with His tender, loving, blessed assurance each night. He is available all day, every day, to me and you, dear friend. Just put Him first. I seek Him with this prayer: "God, help me turn to you first, help me to turn to you always. Help me not ignore my own needs as I desire to help others. Remind me to seek you for help, to ask others for help, and to care for

> **Friend, we can live a life of more if only we make our lives more about Him.**

my whole being—mind, body, and soul. May I be all you created me to be by filling my life with more of you and less of me."

Friend, we can live a life of more if only we make our lives more about Him.

We need to let others know more about Him and His greatness. That what we have–joy, happiness, peace, blessings, and success–are because of Him and not our own works. God will walk us through seasons of pain and struggle to remind us that we need Him and His grace. Our pride closes the door on spiritual growth–I know mine did. The fruits of The Spirit could not grow in my dark, self-sufficient, complacent faith life soil. My life of production, independent of God, was draining. But when I follow Him, seek His wisdom and discernment, and listen to Him, I rest more peacefully. As I grow older (and wiser), I see that I am walking with Jesus in my sufferings. There is such beauty in the dark days. It's hard to compare my sufferings to those of others or become bitter because of them. There is such goodness in all of it if I keep my eyes on Him. Whatever your suffering is—mental illness, infertility, an incurable diagnosis, divorce, poverty—it can be the most precious journey because He is with you.

May we always remember that God wants us—not our work performance, athletic accomplishments, financial statements, or all the accolades, recognition, and praise we get from others. He just wants us. He desires to have all of us in our purest, truest form. He wants our hearts and our minds. May we return to Him again and again what is His anyway–our whole selves. And by returning to Him over and over, may we find strength in Him to do all things. But at the same time, we must remember that just because we CAN do all things, it doesn't mean He has called us to do them. He can and will give us the wisdom, discernment, and courage to say no. Let's lay down our Superman mentalities, which honestly just feed our pride, and only do those things that He calls us to do through Him. Let's find our value and worth in Him, let's rest in Him.

It is an honor to be obedient to Him, make myself more like Him, and rest in Him by honoring the Sabbath. The Sabbath rest is not a day, it is a lifestyle. One that was not easy for me to adopt, and some days (a lot of days!) I struggle to keep a Sabbath lifestyle. I mentioned pride being one of our biggest obstacles to spiritual growth, but so is busyness. We're so busy doing all the things that we don't take time to rest in Him, listen to Him, and prioritize our relationship with Him. I don't know about you, but some days my relationship and reliance on Jesus becomes another piece of the puzzle of my madness: church: check; prayer: check; read my Bible: check. So when this puzzle of madness took over my life–when I allowed myself and my ways to become more and God to become less—He knew the old Jodi needed to "die" so the better me, the person God created me to be, could be "born." And while I felt like everything in my life was falling apart, it was actually all coming together.

And while I felt like everything in my life was falling apart, it was actually all coming together.

I've been living this surrendered life for a handful of years now now, and it feels so good. It's so freeing, but it's also so easy to slip right back into striving and doing all the things. And when I do, which happens often, the fear comes back, the anxiety comes back, and the negative self-talk comes back. Living a surrendered life, making Jesus more, is a constant handing over to Him every day, a constant surrender even multiple times throughout my day. But it helps me remember that I have limitations; I am finite. If want to live my fullest life, I must accept that while I am made in God's image, I am not God. And while I have God-given potential, I also have human limitations.

My prayer for you is that you too would open your palms and surrender your days to Him. We must realize that our worth is in and from Him, not in what we do or produce. We have to realize that we, in

ourselves, will never be
enough. We can never make it
all work out or finish it all
without Him. What we can
do is change our view of what

> **Showing up surrendered,
> with palms wide open, for
> His way is enough.**

is "enough," and I'm here to tell you that a life surrendered to Him makes everything enough. His plan and His purpose for our lives are enough. God makes me enough. Showing up surrendered, with palms wide open, for His way is enough.

You may be wondering if a life surrendered to God will be hard. Yes. My answer is a whole-hearted yes. Life is messy, unpredictable, and just plain hard. God never promised us a carefree, problem-free life. He did promise never to leave our side when faced with the hard days. Having these hard, messy days doesn't mean we are not responsible, productive, or successful, it means we are living life the way God has given it to us. Living our lives as if we have zero limitations is flat-out exhausting. Learning to live with our human limitations and find our strength in Him is rewarding.

Now that I am through the fire of my struggle that brought such restoration and healing, my husband and I can see how God used it all for His glory and the good of others. Mostly the good of Him and our four kids. I carried very heavily the weight of my role as a mom to our four amazing kids. Matt carried the responsibility heavily as well. We have both learned that our roles are not about being the perfect parents or getting all things right all the time. Our role is to love them well, point them to Jesus, and be an example of His love, mercy, grace, patience, and forgiveness. And, as parents, we mustn't underestimate ourselves—our capabilities and our strengths and gifts as parents. God called us to these positions. He chose us for our kids, and He chose them for us. But we can't show them this grace, this mercy, this unconditional love if we are constantly entangled in the knots of perfectionism, performance, managing, and controlling every aspect of our lives.

Friends, let's stop running away from the hard things in life and allow God to use them to transform us spiritually. We must stop turning to things of this world to make us feel good. We must stop turning to our chocolate fixes, our Netflix binges, our endless scrolls on social media, another glass of wine, and getting in on some good gossip—anything and everything to make us feel better, except Him. I believe with my whole heart that my season of anxiety and depression came to be because I was feasting on things of this world—success, performance, pleasing others, accolades, fitting in in all the "right" places—and not on God. It's hard to feast on God's word and His goodness when we feast on things of the world. I was too busy and too preoccupied with managing and living my life to notice what God was trying to do within me. My trial, my struggle, and the valley of death God was taking me through, the Exodus He was exposing me to, was a complete renewal of who I was in Him and in this world. God loves us too much to leave us as we are. If we don't turn to Him, reside in and rely on Him, He will come to refine and restore us in the fire. There is great purpose in His process of pressing and pain.

> **It's hard to feast on God's word and His goodness when we feast on things of the world.**

The parables in the Gospels that talk about fasting at the wedding feast and the old cloth and the wineskins are similar to what God loved me through. He didn't want to simply band-aid or put a patch on my former, self-righteous, self-sufficient self. He could not and would not be combined with my self-righteousness. I was perpetually stuck in my first half-of-life mentality. All I worried about was surviving the day but doing so successfully. I was shuffling through life, thinking my old ways (my wineskins) were good enough, after all, they'd carried me this far. But God was teaching me that my old ways, while still working, were in no way good enough. They could not hold the "new wine" He was attempting to pour into me. He was creating a new wineskin so that it (I) would be strong enough to hold the new wine (ways of life). I had to stretch, and the former me and the way of life I had been living had to replace itself with something better.

Honoring the Sabbath is one way in which I have changed my daily living in order to rest in Him and live a life surrendered to Him. Another way is my regular practice of fasting. When I began to set aside a day for complete rest and Sabbath, and when I started taking breaks from social media, television, podcasts, and foods that gave me a quick fix and spoonful of satisfaction, I began to see that I was turning to Him and His word way more than I ever had before. The first time I fasted with a pure spiritual intention, I was not seeking any kind of physical detox, was in January of 2022, and I experienced spiritual breakthroughs like never before. I had been feeling a call on my heart to write this book and share my story, but I was fearful and also felt ill-equipped and unqualified. But, I wanted to be obedient in listening to what God had placed on my heart. I knew that fasting would prepare the way for God to give me a fresh revelation, fresh vision, and clear purpose. Remember if God is going to pour out new wine, our old wineskins have to go. And well... here I am, writing this book, sharing my story. My fasting includes:

- prayer walks where I fast my lunch and go outside and walk and talk with God
- sun-up to sun-down fasts one day a week
- fasting certain earthly things (i.e. social media, books, news, television, etc.) certain weeks
- prayer focus for my family and friends each week

Fasting in this way, and I don't do it all year long I choose different times of the year to engage in fasting or I do it when I feel God is calling me to it, draws me closer to God, and the closer I am to Him the more fully I am myself. I can move forward in the way He is calling me. I love nothing more than

I love nothing more than finding myself through losing myself in Him.

finding myself through losing myself in Him. When something or someone is weighing heavy on my heart and mind, I will turn to prayer and fasting. When I fast, I am declaring that He is all I need. I am reminding myself that He is my source of strength, hope, faith, and joy. It shows that He is my provision and supplies all I could ever need. He sustains me, He refreshes me, He renews and restores me. A prayer walk during my lunch break at work is far more satisfying, fulfilling, and rejuvenating than any food could ever be.

As I lay down things that aren't serving me, and I spend more time with Him and with these practices of honoring the Sabbath and fasting, I have noticed spiritual breakthroughs. God does not do things for me because I fast, but when I fast, I become more aware of my insufficiencies and need for Him. I become more aware and alert to what He is doing and this creates a desire in me to fast more. As I fill myself up with God, I become increasingly hungry for Him. Jesus can't be added to our work-based ways of life. If we are consumed with our own self-righteousness, there is no room for our faith in Jesus. Life is hard, but our God can and will set us free. Just as He did for David in Psalms 40:2. "He lifted me out of the slimy pit, out of the mud and mire; He set my feet on a rock and gave me a firm place to stand." He rescued me, and He can rescue you too. God provides all we will ever truly need, He sustains us, and He completes us. To have a full, satisfied life, we must crave Him first. We must crave Him most.

To have a full, satisfied life, we must crave Him first. We must crave Him most.

Scripture

Exodus 3:7-8 *"The Lord said, 'I have indeed seen the misery of my people in Egypt. I have heard them crying out because of their slave drivers, and I am concerned about their suffering. So I have come down to rescue them from the hand of the Egyptians and to bring them up out of that land into a good and spacious land, a land flowing with milk and honey...'"*

Psalm 40:2 *"He lifted me out of the slimy pit, out of the mud and mire; he set my feet on a rock and gave me a firm place to stand."*

John 3:30 *"'He must become greater; I must become less.'"*

Reflection

Do you plan and prioritize time with God every day? Do you have alone time with God on a regular basis? What does your time with God look, sound, and feel like? How can you pursue God's peace on purpose?

_____

_____

_____

_____

Prayer

Heavenly Father, thank you for being with us at all times. Even when we are tired, stressed, and full of worries, you give us peace that surpasses all understanding. Please intercede and plant in us a desire to seek you and your wisdom. Calm our racing minds and troubled hearts as you provide us with new mercies each morning. Help us remember that our prayers don't have to be fancy but that calling out to you throughout our day is our best defense. Lord, stir up in us a desire to want you more, to want you most. We trust your love, God, and know that one day we will see you face to face. The joy we now experience by faith will be seen by sight. Amen.

Chapter 10:
Less About The Outcome,
More About The Becoming

In order for God to make us whole, He often has to break us.

I know and trust that God has created each and every one of us for a specific purpose. I also believe that we often don't find our calling, our passion, or our purpose until we have lived, loved, lost, learned, and learned. Often times our calling—our greatest gift to share with others—comes after a season of struggle, heartache, or pain. It's after we've been refined, restored, and renewed that our Creator equips us to guide and mentor others. What we often consider to be the most successful life actually isn't. We have external views and ideas of what success is—career success, ideal husband, and good kids—and we're constantly striving toward greatness. We use a society-created metric to determine our success, but we must remember that life needs to be truly, fully lived. It's not a race we win, and we certainly won't win at life if our concerns are focused on pleasing others before pleasing Him. And in order to please God, we must seek Him, rely on Him, and root our faith and trust in Him. If our faith roots and spiritual lives are rotten, if they are gnarled in the twisted thinking of succeeding, achieving, and obtaining outcomes we have in life, then our lives will be rotten. On the other hand, if our roots are solidly grounded next to streams of living water, if they are firm and connected in a relationship with Jesus, and we're living for what truly matters, then our lives will not only grow, but they will prosper and we will bear fruit. Psalm 1:1-3 says, "Blessed is the one who does not walk in step with the wicked or stand in the way that sinners take or sit in the company of mockers, but whose delight is in the law of the Lord, and who meditates on his law day and night. That person is like a tree planted by streams of water, which yields its fruit in season and whose leaf does not wither—whatever they do prospers."

We need to learn not to spend so much time wishing our lives were different, comparing ourselves to other people or even better versions of ourselves. All lives have good and bad. The hard parts, sadness, failure, and fear are not a result of living a certain way, they just are because we are humans who are actually living. There is no life in a state of sheer happiness at all times—that's not reality, that's not living. If we're living life to the fullest and loving others along the way, we cannot be immune to sadness. Happiness and sadness are woven together; we simply can't experience one without the other. If we compare our lives and judge that we should be happier or someone else is better than us, then we will breed more unhappiness. We need to be all in on the life God has given us, with the people He gifted us with, and live it to the full. If we are fully alive, we can't armor up and protect ourselves from some feelings without closing our hearts to them all.

God uses everything. Nothing is wasted. Every incident we live in and through is intended to bring us closer to Him. He could have fixed my situation quickly, just as the route from Egypt to Israel was only eleven days, but God took the Israelites on the long road, the forty-year journey. And, just as the Israelites wondered, asked, and pleaded, "Why, Lord?" so did I. But I now know, after living through the fire, He needed to really teach me, show me, and see that I was putting all my trust, hope, and faith in Him. If he fixed me quickly, I would have most likely slipped back into my old habits and ways of life—strive, achieve, perform, perfect, control, and survive by sleepwalking through my days. God was breaking me down, testing me, and taking away my foolish, self-sufficient, prideful ways. My sleepless nights, my desperation for something to take away my anxious heart, my searching and seeking for the why and the how were all about Him pointing me back to Him and realizing that all I ever needed or will need is Him. He sustained me just enough–as He did the Israelites with the manna—He made sure I had my daily bread, but He taught me that He was the bread, the truth, and the light I needed. Just as He made sure the Israelites made it to the Promised Land, He made sure I made it through the fiery furnace. But it was not a one-and-done, quick-fix, short-lived journey. Like the Israelites' Exodus, He needed to break open my heart. Rather than allowing me to arrive quickly, He wanted me to be prepared, equipped with His strength and His Word, and built with resilience, tenacity, and endurance in Him—not myself. God did not rush the outcome of my situation even though He could have; instead, He wanted to ensure that I was becoming more like Him.

In transforming us, God often gives us battles that come with wounds so that we really change. We need to be willing to grow and learn, and

> **Like the Israelites, what feels like an exile will become our exodus.**

we do this by carrying whatever cross God has given us to bear. Like the Israelites, what feels like an exile will become our exodus. God knows when it's time for us to wander a bit in the wilderness, but He also promises always to make a parting way for us. What feels like an exile is our good, all-knowing, omnipresent God keeping us from making choices that will lead to our captivity. We must accept that in order for

God to make us whole, He often has to break us. In the breaking, in the crushing, in the pressing, He is rebuilding and reassembling us. He is making new wine. Will we be the same? No. Will we go unscarred? No. But we will be better than ever before.

> **In our becoming, we gain strength, tenacity, perseverance, and hope.**

When we're fighting against life's toughest battles, enduring the pain, the hard, the sad, the hopeless, dark days, we find a way. In our becoming, we gain strength, tenacity, perseverance, and hope. Jesus is our hope, and against all odds, we come out the other side. While we're in the midst of life's storms, we can't see through the muck and mire. We can't fathom that our worst days are setting us up for our best days, but this is the truth of our faith. It is the story of Christ. Jesus' crucifixion and burial, his absolute worst day, led to the resurrection–our

> **We can't fathom that our worst days are setting us up for our best days, but this is the truth of our faith. It is the story of Christ. Jesus' crucifixion and burial, HIS absolute worst day, led to the resurrection–our best day!**

best day! Jesus doesn't just speak light into the darkness; He steps into the darkness. We claw our way out of the valleys, we find something (actually someone–Jesus) deep within our hearts that gives us the will to carry on, to become all He has created us to be. He suffered a criminal's death, a humiliating, lonely, cruel crucifixion on a cross to give us life. Mature believers know that there is a both/and to life—it's called humanity. We are sad and joyful, disappointed and hopeful, sorrowful and grateful. What we cannot afford to do is confuse our life circumstances with our real lives. Something bad may be happening, or we may be enduring a trial that is testing us to our limits, but we are not living bad lives.

Now that I am through my fire, I can look back on the suffering that was, to me at the time, an absolute nightmare and view it as an experience, a transformation, and a spiritual awakening. I can see now that what I thought was a horrible existence and awful life was just a tough time, a trial, a season of struggle. I always say I wouldn't wish what I went through on my worst enemy, but I am glad God took me through it because He renewed, restored, and refined me in the midst of the fire. There is always going to be a part of me that fears going back to that dark, scary place, but if by going back, sharing my story, and reliving it again and again means that others will be helped and others will come out of the darkness with me, then it would be worth it to live it all over again. When we live through seasons of struggle that break us—physically, mentally, emotionally, and spiritually—that's when God's light comes pouring in and shines the brightest. I was praying for change, but I was refusing to get out of God's way. I was self-sufficient and going to fix myself. But God didn't change my circumstance; instead, he used it to change me. The fire of depression and anxiety wasn't burning to destroy me; God was using the flames to refine me.

> But God didn't change my circumstance; instead, He used it to change me. The fire of depression and anxiety wasn't burning to destroy me; God was using the flames to refine me.

My season of pain was so hard, and I hated it, but there was something deep in me that knew He was working in mighty ways. I learned that, in a sense, I had to "die to my old self." I had to be willing to change, to learn, to unlearn, to grow, and to allow others to see the change in me. I had to replace what was no longer serving me or Him well. I had to find what would work well, what would serve me and Him. Some people may call what I went through a "mid-life crisis," but as I've already shared, I like to think of it as more of a spiritual wake-up call or mid-life enlightenment. If we are going to change and experience growth in our lives, if we are going to share our scars and show our battle wounds, we must endure a battle. We then owe it to ourselves and others to pass on the lessons we have learned. Our redemptive stories of survival in seasons of heartache and pain are mostly about how we thrive in the aftermath. One way is to share our struggles and stories, our tests and testimonies, with others. We have loving families and are members of communities that keep us safe, help us feel loved, and we do all we can to keep each other from falling. But the real bond, the truest sense of family and loving one another well, is to show each other that it's okay to fall and need help, and the greatest gift comes in seeing each other get back up—rise and shine again. We need to share our stories, not hide behind them. Sharing our stories is our way of sharing what God has done and is doing in and through us.

> We need to share our stories, not hide behind them. Sharing our stories is our way of sharing what God has done and is doing in and through us.

I, like most people, was living my life invested in the first half—the striving, the seeking, the securing of all the things—family, friends, finances. By my early forties, I thought that was all there was to life. I was worn out and weary. And staying in this pace and way of life kept me in a self-centered frame of mind. I was so afraid of falling, failing, appearing imperfect, or in need of help that I clung to the status quo. Even when, deep down, it was not what was best for me or my loved ones. In my comfortable, familiar way of striving to survive, I would rather stay as I was than face the struggle or have to persevere and endure any change or the thought of that change not working out. By stuffing my feelings away, always needing to have it all together, and being the fixer and denying my pain and anxiety, I was keeping myself from being transformed and renewed by God. My spiritual depths were shallow, and my faith life was complacent and passive. And so God, in His wise, loving ways, walked me into the valley of the shadow of death, and my greatest gain was waiting on the other side of that valley. The growth and close connection that I now have with God came as a result of my time in the valley. I now chase Jesus with my whole heart and mind rather than as an afterthought.

As I am moving into the second half of my life, I am satisfied with not being in control all the time. I have relinquished the idea that I can, or need to, be in charge and manage all the things for all the people. My journey and struggle with anxiety and depression have taught me that life is more about allowing people, circumstances, and happenings around me to teach me how to feel. And I am okay with feeling a gamut of emotions all at once. I am delighted, and I am irritated. I am scared, and I am hopeful. I am sad, and I am joyful. I am nervous, and I am trusting. Along with allowing myself to feel all these feelings, I also allow myself to be influenced by them. I no longer put up this shield to protect my heart. I let it all in, and I let myself feel it all. For I have learned that this is the only true way to live alive. I no longer push down or try to ignore the hard parts of life. I am embracing, feeling, living, exploring, and learning through them. I can no longer carry the weight of stuffing or pretending them away. I have come to realize that my failings and struggles, as well as those of people around me, have the greatest impact and influence on my life. These are the times I have grown and transformed the most. Continuing to live life as if I have no struggles, continuing to ignore the dark pain and suffering of this world, or forging ahead with such certainty that my way is the way would lead nowhere but to my suffering from an inability to trust, know, and connect with myself and others. How can we expect to see, walk into, and soak in the warmth of the light if we haven't experienced the cold, scary loneliness of the dark? There is only one thing, one belief, one person, one Light I can put all my certainty and trust in—that is God. He is The Way, and my certainty in His love for me and my salvation in Him is all I really need. It is all you need too.

We must remove ourselves from calling all the shots, all the ways, all the times. We must surrender to God, we must relinquish control to

SOULFUL SURRENDER

Him- it's where it has always been anyway, so why wear ourselves out
trying to fight it? Have you ever thought maybe you are so tired, so worn
out, and so emotionally drained because you think you are in control? I
encourage you like I have done, to settle into full acceptance of the
Serenity Prayer. Meditating on this prayer has lifted such heavy, self-
inflicted burdens off my shoulders. I no longer desire to change other
people, situations, or circumstances. I am open to God's wisdom to
accept the things I cannot change. I don't obsess over a lack of control. I
am less compulsive in my actions, especially the need and drive to be
doing constantly. I am more settled in what I know I am called to do,
and I am done worrying about the consequences. I am okay with being
delighted by others and outcomes, and I know I will be okay when the
outcomes of life happenings make me sad or scared. As I am becoming
all that God has made me to be, I am learning that the outcome doesn't
really matter. I don't need to compete; there is no need to be better,
flashier, or more impressive than others. I can just be me. I am living out
my life in full acceptance of who I am, and the job I have done or haven't
done, and I am fully embracing that my light comes from Jesus within
me, and that is all the light I need. My days are not wrapped up in
winning, doing, and getting it all right. But rather, I can feel that through
my time in prayer and reading His Word, I am gaining wisdom and
discernment. My responses to life happenings and what others say or do
to me are more reflective. I no longer have the desire to change,
manipulate, or persuade. I am learning to accept. Friend, I encourage you
to do the same. Lay it all down. Give it to Jesus. And, if you're anything
like me, you'll take it back again and again, but He will be there, arms
wide open when you're ready to surrender it again. So do it; give it all
back to Him as many times as it takes. You won't regret it.

I used to carry a lot of guilt, embarrassment, and shame about my
~~breakdown~~ breaking open. But now I accept my falling down, and I
embrace the imperfections. This acceptance allows me to be open and
accepting of others who fall or who may let me down. And I often
wonder, would I have risen if I hadn't fallen? Would I have transformed?

158

Would I have grown? Would I have become all that He wants me to be? Or would I have kept controlling, managing, and manipulating life so that I would get the perfect outcome? I know deep in the depths of my soul that I was so obsessive and compulsive about controlling and managing all the things because I was trying to avoid natural life sufferings, sufferings that are just a part of life because we are human. By doing so, I brought on more painful suffering. My insomnia, anxiety, and depression crept in as slowly and stealthily as a snake while I was so focused on dodging the bullets of pain that come from everyday, ordinary human living.

It was a true gift God did not continue to reward my drive. He had to bring me to the absolute end of myself so that I could find Him. I had to learn to let go of everything in my life—the striving, performing, pleasing—and hold on to only Him. He had work to do in and through me for His glory and honor. I had to learn not to strive in the name of Jesus but rather relish in the good work He was doing in my life. I had to learn, and most days I am still learning this, that I am not here to manage and manipulate all the outcomes. I am here to become. Wanting to be in control doesn't make me freakish; it makes me human. But managing our lives and living them are two completely different things. I was in a perpetual state of managing my life, and I have learned to be much happier simply by living it. When we're all in, fighting for all the things, we easily lose sight of what truly matters. Take it from me, those small, daily things that seem so big, so important, they just aren't. Let yourself stop, rest, observe, and just be. Don't wait until you're exhausted or find yourself breaking apart to care for yourself. Listen to your heart, mind, and soul. Look for and listen to Jesus. He is tending to you all along the way. He is with you in your becoming.

When I took time away from work to seek the rest and medical attention I desperately needed, I remember being at home day after pain-staking day asking, "Why, God, why?" But my question should have been, "Why not?" I'm a human; suffering is part of this life journey. Other people have suffered around me over various struggles in life for years, so why would I think that I would journey through this life unscathed, on a perfect path of peace with no struggles, challenges, or obstacles? In order to begin true mental, emotional, and spiritual healing, I had to reframe my thinking and questioning from "Why me?" to "Why not me?" If we live life long enough, we will encounter suffering, and we will learn that sometimes God has to allow the bad, hurtful ways of life to happen so that He can accomplish His good work. His strength is seen in our weakness. His goodness abounds in all the bad. His light shines brightest in the darkness. In my becoming, I am learning that God often does not fix us or our circumstances immediately. When we are devastated, frustrated, worr-ied, and feeling completely hopeless, He is reaching in and doing some of His best work. His light shines through all of our shattered, broken places. He knows that a quick fix won't last. After all, we're human and our tendencies to slide backward are too tempting. He uses our seasons of struggle to show us that surrendering our lives to Him is the only way to live fully and freely alive. In my soulful surrender, I have been made stronger as I allow Him to work in me so I can become everything He created me to be. I can now see that beauty does come from ashes, and there is beauty in brokenness. I believe with my whole heart that God used my anxiety and depression to slow me

> If we live life long enough, we will encounter suffering, and we will learn that sometimes God has to allow the bad, hurtful ways of life to happen so that He can accomplish His good work. His strength is seen in our weakness. His goodness abounds in all the bad. His light shines brightest in the darkness.

down—even stop me. He used that time to turn my eyes toward Him, to teach me how to be still and know that He is God. It was in this time that I learned how to lay it all down at His feet and unburden myself. And one finger at a time, I released my white-knuckle, jaw-clinching grip and opened my palms to Him in surrender. I encourage you to open your palms as well. Let go. Let God do the kind of work only He can do.

Let go. Let God do the kind of work only He can do.

I now know better how to live fully alive, accepting that there will always be hard, messy stuff in my life. But instead of stuffing it down, ignoring it, pretending it away, or striving to fix it all, I give myself, others, and each day grace as they come. Things don't get better by being ignored or fixed; they get better by being recognized and accepted. What I can do, what I am trying to do, and what I hope you'll do too with your own story is acknowledge and celebrate the strength and wisdom I have gained through my suffering. I am by no means fixed or fine. I have not arrived. But I have grown, and I am strong. And I am grateful to know that whatever storms may come my way, I have an Almighty God who is going to see me through, and I have peace and hope running deep in my soul. I don't want to go back to before my breaking open and soulful surrender. I have moments, still, where I fear that I will slip back to that way of thinking, that way of being, that way of living, striving, and performing. And I don't want to go back there. That season of struggle, the daily battles, and the war that seemed to rage endlessly have brought me to where I am today and who I am—fully myself, fully with God. But I know deep in my heart that I can never, I will never, go all the way back there. Everything I learned about myself and the goodness of God will keep me from ever going all the way back. Might I have seasons of struggle, days filled with anxious thoughts, times of sadness, and even depression? Yes. For sure. I will face those times again, I have no doubt. It was during my season of being home alone, trying to work through my anxiety and depression, that I learned how to lose my life and truly give it to God. God met me and started to pull back the layers and revealed to me how I had been living all along was not the way to live, and He showed me, "For whoever wants to save their life will lose it, but whoever loses their life for me will find it" (Matthew 16:25). So while I know I will face more challenging times during my life on this earth, I also have no doubt that I have a Lord of love and He will never leave me or forsake me.

I did not set out on writing this book to give you a well-planned road map or five-step plan on how to do less in order to live and feel more. This was never my plan because I don't have the magic answer—I don't hold the key that unlocks all the worry, strife, and struggle. Learning to do less—to surrender to God—is not easy. It's certainly not pretty, and it's not a linear path. It is hard. It is messy. It is an arduous, contorted, and oftentimes confusing journey. I fell down, and for every step I took forward, there were often two, three, four, or more steps back. I felt off balance, out of place, and out of control. Because I am out of control—we all are. Remember, control has never been ours. It's always belonged to Him.

> **Remember, control has never been ours. It's always belonged to Him.**

There is no right way to transform, learn, and grow. But what I can tell you is that it's about hope. It's about allowing yourself to have the space and willingness to change, grow, and let go. It's about surrender. God told me, showed me, how to slow down. I was doing things for me; my performance equaled accolades thrown my way. I had to be slowed down—no, I had to be stopped—so I could ask what I was doing for Him. Am I living a life that points others to Jesus?

Was my ~~breakdown~~ breaking open easy? Was it rewarding, invigorating, and inspiring? No way. Not at all. Not even close. But I had to feel the pain of the valley that my choices had led me into. There is, after all, power in the pain. There is great growth that comes from sitting in the brokenness, from being present in the becoming. I was not self-centered and focused on what was going to be my reward at the end of the grueling pain. I was present and focused on what each day of the journey would give me. I realized that with each new day and the mercies He was giving me, God was not about to leave me in the dark. He would not leave me in the valley. He was using the pain of my performing, achieving, and getting the job done at all costs to show me how off course I really was. He was not going to take the pain away, but He was using the pain to equip me with the tools I needed to find my way out.

Now, more than six years later, I do not have a life free from problems or worrisome days. I still find myself slipping into states of fear, sadness, despair, frustration, anxiety, irritability, bitterness, and rage. But the difference is that I no longer question myself, my faith, or God's love for me. Instead, I realize these are times when I need to continue to seek Him with intention. I need to surrender myself and my feelings to Him again and again. I am more accepting of myself as a human that has fragmented feelings, emotions, and reactions. Until my time on this earth has expired, I will always have weaknesses and be in a state of brokenness. And I am okay with that because His love and light shine the brightest through the cracks of my life. And, by accepting my various levels and degrees of brokenness and weakness, I am more acutely aware of my need for Him.

While I am so much better, physically, emotionally, relationally, and spiritually, than I was in 2017, the world is still the same broken, disappointing, messed up place it's always been. I have resigned to the idea of the perfect outcome, the perfect life. Instead, I have learned to embrace learning, growing, unlearning, and becoming who He wants me to be. I am focused on how He is working in and through me so that I may become all He wants me to be. I now seek, crave, and desire solitude and introversion. My life has been active, busy, hurried, and stimulated enough. Now I can sit back, evaluate, process, and integrate it all. I enjoy how I see things differently now. I am moving through life at a slower pace, and it's amazingly beautiful. The little things are becoming more important to me. The everyday, ordinary happenings are what matter most. A part of me wishes they would have always captivated me in this way. But then I realized if they always delighted and impressed me, they wouldn't as much now. God has been writing the words of my story and now He is helping me examine, explain, and reflect on my story. It is an interesting, rewarding, and soulful practice. I no longer strive to do more, be more, or have more. I don't seek to obtain what I love. I now sink into loving what I have always had.

> **I no longer strive to do more, be more, or have more. I don't seek to obtain what I love. I now sink into loving what I have always had.**

God knows that when we face fear, we become fearless. He takes our lives on journeys where we have to face our fears. Then He brings us through; He did for me and will for you too. God doesn't highlight the areas in our lives where we are strong and view Him as unnecessary. He works in the areas of our lives where we are weak so that He can highlight His strength. He uses our sufferings not only to grow us but also to help others. Once we get through whatever our "it" is, our difficult times, we can help someone else through it. And that is exactly why I am writing this book. I am carrying what God has given me up the mountain, and I am sharing my story for the good of others and glory to Him. God led me out of my Egypt into His Promised Land, and He will lead you too. I am being obedient to what God has called me to do. I am determined to help others find their way out of the darkest valley.

The world needs more of who we are becoming regardless of who we have been in the past. I am becoming someone who hopes for the best but doesn't have a need to be the best. I'm becoming someone who is releasing the need for control and surrendering and trusting God more with the outcome. I am

> **The world needs more of who we are becoming regardless of who we have been in the past.**

becoming less of a should-do person and becoming more of a could-do person. And during my journey these last six years, I became someone who started taking yoga classes, and now I have become someone who teaches yoga and shares with others how they can more intimately connect with God during their yoga practice. I became someone who discovered joy in writing in my journal, and now I have become someone who publishes some of my work. I became, and am still becoming, someone who puts God first every day rather than as an afterthought, admired and thanked in a rushed prayer at the end of a busy day. I used to be someone who found pride in a jam-packed, busy schedule and calendar, and now I am becoming someone who is over-the-moon at the thought of staying home and catching up on some much-needed rest. Who were you, friend? Who are you becoming?

I hold no shame about the person I was before because she is the one who carried and led me to the person I am today. Throughout my soulful surrender, God has been teaching me that life is less about the outcome and more about the becoming. The person I am becoming, the person you are becoming, is who God always intended us to be, and He has loved us all along the way. Let's surrender our worries, fears, and all of our days to Him. Let's become someone who does less, so God can do more.

Let's become someone who does less, so God can do more.

Scripture

1 Corinthians 3:18 *"Do not deceive yourselves. If any of you think you are wise by the standards of this age, you should become "fools" so that you may become wise."*

Acts 4:11 *"Jesus is 'the stone you builders rejected, which has become the cornerstone.'"*

Proverbs 13:20 *"Walk with the wise and become wise, for a companion of fools suffers harm."*

Reflection

What, in your life, can you do less of so God can do more? Where in your life can you let go, release, surrender, and just be? Which of the chapters in this book will help you to be less worried about the outcome and more focused on becoming?

_____

_____

_____

_____

Prayer

Dear Lord, as we strive to become more like Jesus, give us the wisdom to know that we will encounter bumps and obstacles along the way. Give us the discernment to know when to move forward and when to pause, surrender and wait for you. Lord, as we encounter and work through life's many challenges, help us to remember that the race of life is not about our swiftness but more about our willingness to lean and rely on you. Give us the perseverance, strength, and endurance to see our trials through, with you, to the end.

NOTES

Chapter 1: Less Doing, More "Be"ing

1. Jennifer Dukes Lee, Growing Slow (Grand Rapids, MI: Zondervan, 2021), 172.

2. Jennifer Dukes Lee, Growing Slow (Grand Rapids, MI: Zondervan, 2021), 174.

Chapter 2: Less Yes, More No

1. Brene Brown, Ph.D., L.M.S.W., The Gifts Of Imperfection (Center City, MN: Hazelden, 2010), 101.

2. Brene Brown, Ph.D., L.M.S.W., The Gifts Of Imperfection (Center City, MN: Hazelden, 2010), 1.

3. Eckhart Tolle, The Power Of Now (Vancouver, BC: Namaste, 1999), 213.

Chapter 4: Less Striving, More Thriving

1. Brene Brown, Ph.D., L.M.S.W., The Gifts Of Imperfection (Center City, MN: Hazelden, 2010), 55-58.

Chapter 8: Less Fitting In, More Belonging

1. Eckhart Tolle, The Power Of Now (Vancouver, BC: Namaste, 1999), 216.

2. Lisa Whittle, Jesus Over Everything, Women Limiting Women. Podcast audio. October 12, 2022. https://open.spotify.com/episode/7bMxXYD4wRYVmp5hc DQ3wo.

Acknowledgments

This book would not have been possible without the love, support, encouragement, and prayers of so many. I am forever grateful for the following people who helped make this book a reality:

Jesus Christ, my Lord and Savior. Thank you for going before me and showing me the way. You flung doors wide open for this process in the most unexpected and unimaginable ways. You never cease to amaze me. None of this would be possible without you. I give you all the glory and honor.

Matthew, my husband, best friend, biggest supporter, and number one fan. Thank you for taking my hand in yours and walking through the fire with me. Thank you for always believing in me when I forget to believe in myself. And thank you for your love and faithfulness for God and me; it has blessed me over and over.

My kids Anna, Jack, Abby, and Maggie, being your mom has grown me in countless ways. Along with your dad, you are my life's greatest gifts. I am so grateful that God chose us for each other. I am better because of you. I look forward to seeing all the beautiful ways God will work in your lives. Never forget He is always with you and for you.

Mom and Dad, words are not enough to express my endless gratitude to you for raising me in a safe, loving home, where you always modeled and shared your love for Jesus. Thank you for teaching and showing me The Way.

My book prayer team, there are too many of you to name, but you know who you are. Thank you for your endless support and encouragement. Thank you for uttering prayers for me, and this book, when I was unable to form the words myself.

To Called Creatives, thank you for providing a welcoming, supportive, Christ-centered coaching community for women who want to share Jesus with the world. I cannot thank you enough for believing in me and helping me turn my story into a book for others to hold. A special thanks to Jess Carey, Elise Daly-Parker, and Michele Wilbert, members of my Mastermind group and the dearest of friends. If it weren't for your cheerleading and words of wisdom, I'm not sure I would have been brave enough to begin this journey.

About The Author

Jodi Kinasewitz is passionate about helping others build a life that is based on mental and spiritual wellness. She is dedicated to sharing her story of struggle through a difficult and dark season of insomnia, anxiety, and depression. When she is not teaching her elementary students how to read, Jodi loves to travel with her family and she spends any time she can outdoors. Jodi has had several articles published on various Christian platforms, she was published in the *Milk & Honey Women Devotional Journal*, Volume 1, and most recently she co-authored and published a devotional journal titled *Unshakable Peace in an Unsteady World*. Jodi's hope is that by sharing her story, her writing will shine a light on the importance of mental health while pointing her readers to Jesus.

.

www.ingramcontent.com/pod-product-compliance
Lightning Source LLC
Chambersburg PA
CBHW031523120626
46545CB00005B/1966

* 9 7 8 1 9 6 1 7 3 2 0 7 0 *